TWAYNE'S WORLD AUTHORS SERIES

A Survey of the World's Literature

Sylvia E. Bowman, Indiana University
GENERAL EDITOR

GERMAN LITERATURE

Ulrich Weisstein, Indiana University
EDITOR

Drama of the Storm and Stress

(TWAS 83)

TWAYNE'S WORLD AUTHORS SERIES (TWAS)

The purpose of TWAS is to survey the major writers —novelists, dramatists, historians, poets, philosophers, and critics—of the nations of the world. Among the national literatures covered are those of Australia, Canada, China, Eastern Europe, France, Germany, Greece, India, Italy, Japan, Latin America, New Zealand, Poland, Russia, Scandinavia, Spain, and the African nations, as well as Hebrew, Yiddish, and Latin Classical literatures. This survey is complemented by Twayne's United States Authors Series and English Authors Series.

The intent of each volume in these series is to present a critical-analytical study of the works of the writer; to include biographical and historical material that may be necessary for understanding, appreciation, and critical appraisal of the writer; and to present all material in clear, concise English—but not to vitiate the scholarly content of the work by doing so.

Drama of the Storm and Stress

By MARK O. KISTLER

Other Twayne's World Authors Series Books on German Literature Include:

ERNST BARLACH, Edson M. Chick

SEBASTIAN BRANT, Edwin H. Zeydel

FRIEDRICH DURRENMATT, Murray B. Peppard

MAX FRISCH, Ulrich Weisstein

GUNTER GRASS, W. Gordon Cunliffe

FRIEDRICH HEBBEL, Sten G. Flygt

HEINRICH MANN, Rolf N. Linn

THOMAS MANN, Ignace Feuerlicht

FERDINAND RAIMUND, John Michalski

ANGELUS SILESIUS, Jeffrey Sammons

RICHARD WAGNER, Robert Raphael

FRANK WEDEKIND, Sol Gittleman

WALTHER VON DER VOGELWEIDE, George F. Jones

Twayne Publishers, Inc. :: New York

Preface

This is the first monograph in English on the German "Sturm und Drang" ("Storm and Stress") drama which includes a detailed analysis of the major plays of the period. The two longer studies in English—H. B. Garland's *Storm and Stress* and Roy Pascal's *The German Sturm und Drang*—embrace all genres and the various phases of the age of genius, with the consequence that neither work is able to devote more than two pages to any one play. Pascal, by his own admission, did not aim "to analyze the poetic qualities of the imaginative works of the Sturm und Drang," but rather confined himself to painting the composite intellectual, sociological, religious, historical, and esthetic backdrop against which the works of art were written. I am greatly indebted to one essay in English, "J. M. R. Lenz" (Chapter One in Max Spalter's study, *Brecht's Tradition*), for giving me perspective in writing a modern interpretation of *Der Hofmeister* and *Die Soldaten*. Of books in German, F. J. Schneider's *Die deutsche Dichtung der Geniezeit* provides brief but modern insights into the chief plays of concern to us here. The major books on "Storm and Stress" dramatists, written at the end of the nineteenth century, are quite outdated. A number of doctoral dissertations, treating various aspects of the plays, were written in the twentieth century, but they are of uneven quality. One recent critical work—Christoph Hering's *Friedrich Maximilian Klinger*—was helpful, although it is primarily concerned with Klinger's post "Storm and Stress" output.

The "Storm and Stress" drama deserves a reappraisal. Today, when traditional mores, social institutions, and art forms are the object of critical scrutiny, and when the discrepancies of the human condition are viewed existentially, the age of genius, as a similarly oriented time, takes on especial significance and warrants renewed attention.

In my analyses, I have quoted liberally from the dramas and from the authors' diaries, thus allowing the writers to speak for themselves. For the most part, I have translated the quotations which appear in the text. In those instances where the eccentricities in style and vocabulary are integrally related to the dramatists' artistic purpose, I have allowed the German to stand.

I am grateful to my colleagues, William N. Hughes and Stuart A. Gallacher, for their reading of my manuscript and their many helpful suggestions. Finally, I want to express my thanks for receiving a research grant from Michigan State University, which enabled me to travel to other university libraries to use their materials.

Contents

DRAMA OF THE
STORM AND STRESS
by
MARK O. KISTLER

Although the Storm and Stress period of German literature was short-lived, reaching its peak in the middle of the 1770's, its dramas have had considerable influence on later literary movements, particularly in modern times. Professor Kistler pays special attention to the works of J. M. R. Lenz, which have influenced Brecht and his disciples. Lenz's plays, filled with social outrage and at the same time with the ironic nature of human striving, attain a new relevance today. In matters of technique as well, Lenz's episodic structure and F. M. Klinger's highly charged, emotional style have left their mark on twentieth century drama.

The author gives a detailed analysis of the major dramas of Lenz and Klinger, as well as those of H. L. Wagner, Maler Müller, and J. A. Leisewitz. Wagner is a precursor of Naturalism by writing socially oriented plays which depict in sympathetic and minute detail the milieu of the common people. Typical of the young geniuses of Storm and Stress, Müller, especially in his *Faust,* gives fine poetic expression to ebullient, Promethean man who would remove the shackles imposed on him by fate and tradition in order to realize his potential.

Chronology

1747   H. L. Wagner born in Strassburg.

1749   Goethe born in Frankfurt. Maler Müller born in Kreuznach (Palatinate).

1751   J. M. R. Lenz born in Sesswegen (Livonia).

1752   Klinger born in Frankfurt. Leisewitz born in Hannover.

1766   Müller goes to Zweibrücken to be apprenticed as painter.

1768   Lenz matriculates at the University of Königsberg as a student of theology; he comes under Kant's and Hamann's influence.

1770   Leisewitz enters the University of Göttingen; and meets members of Hainbund and Lessing.

1771   Lenz arrives in Strassburg and remains there until 1776; he meets Goethe. Wagner makes Goethe's acquaintance in the winter of 1770/71; he studies at the local university. Leisewitz begins writing *Julius von Tarent*.

1773   Wagner accepts a position as tutor in Saarbrücken.

1774   Publication of Lenz's *Anmerkungen übers Theater, Der Hofmeister, Der neue Menoza*, and *Lustpiele nach dem Plautus fürs deutsche Theater*. Müller meets Charlotte Kärner and leaves for Mannheim. Klinger, with financial assistance from Goethe, goes to the University of Giessen to study law. Leisewitz returns to Hannover and finishes *Julius von Tarent*.

1775   Lenz is visited by Goethe in Strassburg—a climax in their relationship; he writes *Pandaemonium Germanicum* as a tribute to Goethe. Publication of Wagner's *Prometheus, Deukalion, und die Rezensenten, Der wohltätige Unbekannte*, and *Die Reue nach der Tat*. Müller makes Goethe's acquaintance in Mannheim; he begins to work on *Golo und Genoveva* and *Fausts Leben;* he writes *Die Schafschur, Der erschlagene Abel, Der Satyr Mopsus*, and *Bacchidon und Milon*. Publication of Klinger's *Otto* and *Das leidende Weib*. Klinger writes *Die neue Arria* and *Die Zwillinge*. Leisewitz writes *Die Pfändung* and *Der Besuch um Mitternacht*.

1776   Lenz in Weimar from April until December. Publication of *Die Soldaten, Die beiden Alten,* and *Die Freunde machen den Philosophen.* Publication of Wagner's *Neuer Versuch über die Schauspielkunst* and *Die Kindsmörderin.* Wagner settles in Frankfurt and marries, but his wife dies in 1778. Müller meets Wagner, Lenz, and Klinger. Publication of his *Situation aus Fausts Leben* and the scenes "Genoveva im Turme" and "Die Pfalzgräfin Genoveva." Publication of Klinger's *Die Zwillinge, Die neue Arria,* and *Simsone Grisaldo.* Klinger writes *Sturm und Drang,* visits Goethe in Weimar, and joins the Seyler theater company in October. Publication of Leisewitz' *Julius von Tarent* without the author's consent.

1777   Publication of Lenz's *Der Engländer;* Lenz suffers his first attack of madness. Publication of Wagner's *Briefe, die Seylersche Schauspielergesellschaft betreffend.* Wagner joins the Seyler theater company. Klinger writes *Stilpo und seine Kinder.* Publication of his *Sturm und Drang.*

1778   Publication of Wagner's *Voltaire am Abend seiner Apotheose.* Müller writes *Adams erstes Erwachen und erste selige Nächte* and *Niobe.* He leaves Mannheim for Rome. Klinger becomes an officer in the Austrian army. Leisewitz enters the administration of the Duchy of Braunschweig.

1779   Lenz returns to Riga. Wagner dies on March 4 at the age of thirty-two.

1780   Publication of Klinger's *Stilpo und seine Kinder.* Klinger obtains a commission in the Russian army and goes to Russia. Leisewitz meets Goethe in Weimar.

1792   Lenz dies in Moscow.

1806   Leisewitz dies.

1811   Müller's *Golo und Genoveva* and *Das Nusskernen* published.

1825   Müller dies in Rome.

1831   Klinger dies in Russia.

CHAPTER 1

The Literary Forebears

THE literary movement known as the Storm and Stress possesses an individuality and significance which have not been fully appreciated until our time. Strangely enough, the movement was only of brief duration. Although it is imprudent to define its strict limits, its main creations originated between 1770 and 1780. In fact, the dramas that are treated in this study were all written within the space of five years, namely between 1771 and 1776.

The "Storm and Stress" was a revolt of youth against the established ideas and values of the Age of Reason. These angry young men who banded together in a cult of genius seriously questioned the traditional eighteenth-century belief in the intellectual and moral perfectibility of mankind through cultural progress. For them Leibnitz' teleology and its attendant message of optimism no longer rang true. Basically, the "Storm and Stress" attacked the idea that man's reason held the clue to his ultimate salvation; rather, the cult of genius believed that man's subjective element revealed his true, creative nature. One began to glorify the irrational aspect of man with particular emphasis on the development of the emotional, imaginative, mysterious, and occult faculties. Philosophical thought and elaborate systems of rules were relegated to a position of obscurity in favor of man's reliance on his feelings, desires, and natural urges—in short, his genius. No longer did "polite society," in which the aristocracy was dominant, determine the cultural tone; on the contrary, the "Storm and Stress" sought its destiny in the primitive, in the origins of civilization, among the simple, innocent folk who lived in harmony with nature.

Even before 1770, signs of a new outlook could be detected. The Swiss scientist and poet, Albrecht von Haller, in his descriptive poem "Die Alpen" (1734), detects innocence among the Alpine peasants who live in a remote area where civilization has not yet penetrated. In Haller's poem, as well as in J. G. Schnabel's *Die Insel Felsenburg* (1731–43) and Salomon Gessner's *Idyllen* (1756), mankind flees the evils and vices of the city and finds an idyllic life in an unspoiled rural habitat.

I   French and English Influences

That the writers just mentioned were forerunners of the "Storm and Stress," there can be no doubt. But at the middle of the eighteenth century, when German literature was held in disrepute in Germany itself, it was the foreign—particularly the French and English—sources which effectively promoted the revolutionary ideas. It was especially the writings of Jean-Jacques Rousseau which dramatically changed the mode of thinking in the age of Enlightenment. Completely disillusioned by the social atmosphere of the Rococo, Rousseau attacked contemporary society in particular and civilization in general for alienating man from his natural state. Counterbalancing this denunciation, he praised the simple peasant, the young child, the "noble savage," and all manner of primitive peoples. Only with primal innocence could one overcome the wicked refinements and artificialities of the contemporary pseudo-civilization. What further impressed the young German revolutionaries in Rousseau's doctrine was his advocacy of a natural religion. For even though German youth rebelled, at times, against God, they never denied the divine and were avowed enemies of materialistic atheism. Rousseau castigated manmade laws and the fruits of pure intellect. In *La nouvelle Héloïse* and the *Confessions* he based ethics on the emotional, intuitive, autonomistic nature of the human being. Rousseau considered feeling more genuine than reason. If man's feelings were intense and he followed his heart, he could not help but achieve his destiny. It was these ideas which provided the "Storm and Stress" writers with a justification for their exaggerated cult of feeling. Self-indulgent, undisciplined, impulsive man was to replace the one dictated by reason and intellect.

Although Rousseau had perhaps the greatest single influence on the Storm and Stress, it was a group of English writers who had a similarly astonishing impact on the revolutionary movement. Thus Edward Young, mainly because of his rhapsodic essay entitled *Conjectures on Original Composition* (1759), left a greater impression on German than on English literature. The concept of the artist as genius who creates altogether independently of manmade rules stems, to a great extent, from Young. On the one hand, he likens an "original" poet to a plant which rises spontaneously from the vital root of genius; which grows and is not made. On the other hand, he ascribes to the artist genius a transcendental nature. Genius is man filled with God, a second creator, a true Prometheus. In any event, Young emphasizes the spontaneity and irrationality of original creation, distinguishing sharply between original creativity and manufactured work. If one must imitate, Young says, one should imitate the method of a genius such as Homer, not the *Iliad*, his product. In more modern times, Shakespeare is, for Young, the supreme genius; and the translation of *Conjectures on Original Composition* represents an important turn in Shakespeare appreciation in Germany.

To be sure, Shakespeare was not unknown in German letters in the middle of the eighteenth century. Companies of English players performed his works, although crudely, and attempts were made to translate some dramas, and poets like Johann Elias Schlegel wrote with appreciation of his works; but it was not until Young's emotionally charged dithyrambics in praise of Shakespeare made their impact felt in Germany that a true Shakespeare cult developed. This deification of Shakespeare persisted until the age of Romanticism and, to a certain extent, is still in evidence down to the present. It mattered little that the Storm and Stress image of Shakespeare was a woefully distorted one. The important thing is that the English dramatist became a symbol of genius itself, a powerful Titan who creates spontaneously and demonically, completely impervious to established rules and traditions. One venerated the violence and highly charged rhetoric of *King Lear*, the bloodthirsty intrigues and unbridled passion of the historical dramas, and the seemingly utter disregard of the unities, while failing to see the inner unity and purpose of the individual dramas.

To some extent, the false conception of Shakespeare was due to inadequacies in the first extensive translation into German— that of Wieland. Wieland published seventeen of the plays under the title of *Shakespeares Theatralische Werke*. Except for *A Midsummer Night's Dream*, all appeared in prose. It goes without saying that a prose version could not do justice to Shakespeare's poetic language, and Wieland was severely criticized for his efforts, by Gerstenberg among others. Nevertheless, it is to Wieland's credit that he made Shakespeare accessible to German men of letters in the latter half of the eighteenth century, and that, inept as his translations may be, enough of the greatness came through to inspire a whole generation of poets.

If Shakespeare was the idol of the young "geniuses," so was the Gaelic bard, Ossian. Even though today we regard Ossianic poems as a literary oddity, as a wistful creation of Macpherson's pen to breathe new life into an age long gone by, the salient point is that the Storm and Stress poets considered these Gaelic poems to be the genuine expression of a primitive poet. The wild battle songs and the heroic pose in this early Scottish poetry corresponded to the manly, combative spirit of the young men of the 1770's. In like manner, the propensity for the mysterious and the occult, as well as for the mood of the foggy landscape, imparted to the German poets an atmosphere which they found conducive to inspired poetic creativity. The Scottish landscape became popular and influenced the nature concept—more so than Haller's and Rousseau's Alpine sceneries. The traditional gently rolling Rococo landscape with its flowering meadows, babbling brooks, shady groves, singing birds, and grazing herds was now replaced by the gloomy coasts and the desolate heath, and the eternally cheerful spring of the earlier poetry by rainstorms and thunder showers.

II *German Precursors*

One poet particularly attracted to this type of landscape was a German precursor of the Storm and Stress, Klopstock. His *Hermanns Schlacht* (1769) was interspersed with bardic songs in the Ossianic tradition and helped promote serious interest among the German people in their past. Because of his subject matter, dealing with national themes and patriotic enthusiasm, and particularly because of the image of the poet he projected, the Storm and Stress regarded him as a prophet and leader. Klopstock was the first German to deify the office of the poet, and he regarded his mission as a privileged and sacred one in the service of the Almighty. Unlike in the earlier age of Rationalism, when writing creatively was a favorite pastime, it was the purpose of life itself, which prompted a feeling of self-reverence within the poet, raising him above the norms of ordinary mortals. This new interpreation of the artist-genius had a lasting affect on German letters, making a particular impression, even after the 1770's, on Classicism and Romanticism.

The great esteem in which the admirers of genius held Klopstock can be demonstrated graphically by quoting a passage from Herder's postscript to his essay *Uber Ossian und die Lieder alter Völker*. Praising Klopstock's poetry, Herder says:

> It is a sevenfold source . . . if the full, healthy bloom of the world's youth can and is to be renewed, so *that in ode and grace at table, in hymn and love-song, the heart will speak, and no code of rules, no Horace, Pindar, or Orbilius.
>
> Ode! It becomes again what it was! The feeling of a total situation of life! Dialogue of the human heart—with God! With itself! With all nature.
>
> Euphony! It becomes again what it was. Not an artificial construction of numbered harmonies! Movement! Melody of the heart! Dance![1]

Herder's staccato, dithyrambic style employed in this quotation conveys the highly charged emotional effect which Klopstock's poetry exerted. The phrase, "dialogue of the human heart—with God!" (Gespräch Menschlichen Herzens—mit Gott!) is particularly revealing, for here Herder pays homage to Klopstock's attempt to recapture for the heart the vast area of religion traditionally controlled by the theologian and moralist. Not only religion but all of life was suddenly freed from the unsympathetic intellect, in order that inclinations, sentiments, and emotions could reign supreme to lead man to his true potential.

The same obedience to the heart, rather than to the rule of reason, permeates the writings of Johann Georg Hamann, who qualifies as the immediate forerunner of the Storm and Stress movement. A wayward genius, he was a man of strange complexity: a frustrated government clerk in Königsberg and a Bohemian nonconformist; a deeply religious person who never bothered to marry the mother of his children; a seer and, at the same time, a satyr. He wrote in an obscure, oracular style with a penchant for expressing his ideas in fragmentary and aphoristic form, and his sibylline utterances made him popular with the new generation of revolutionary writers. Like Rousseau and Young, he would also seek his inspiration among primitive peoples, but instead of merely going back to the European folk songs and folk literature, or to the ancient Greeks, he would restore poetry through the imitation of Oriental poetry, primarily that of the Old Testament. Using the Bible as his guide, Hamann asserted that all phenomenal reality exists only if it is divinely created. All creation is revelation; and through creation God makes Himself manifest to man. Not only are all created tangibles divine, but so are the senses perceiving them. Nature works through the senses and passions, but unfortunately the age of Rationalism had stifled this aspect of man. Hamann wanted man to use his passions as he uses his limbs, in order to penetrate to his inner creative power. In this respect he says in his cabalistic rhapsody, *Aesthetica in nuce*, which appeared as part of the *Kreuzzüge des Philologen* (1762):

Use your passions, as you use your limbs.... Passion alone gives abstractions, as well as hypotheses, hands, feet, and wings—metaphors and symbols impart spirit, life, and speech.... My coarse power of phantasy has never been able to imagine a creative spirit without genitalia.[2]

The last sentence reveals another interesting aspect of Hamann's nature, the baroque-like polarity of his images. As in this instance, he often combined devout religious sentiment with the most sensual idiom. Sexual functions may not be delicate, but to Hamann they were the expression and symbol of creativeness. The sensual and emotional aspects of Hamann's views derive largely from his pietistic upbringing, with its emphasis on the intimate, personal relation to God.

This desire to get to the heart of things by relying on instinct rather than on intellect is also the motivating idea in Hamann's *Sokratische Denkwürdigkeiten* (1759). According to Hamann, Socrates was ignorant not out of stupidity but because of his sensitivity. Hamann further asserts that between sensitivity and doctrine there is a greater difference than between a living animal and its skeleton. It is views like these which anticipate Herder and the young Goethe. The entire Storm and Stress period drew creative inspiration from the contrast between doctrine and life. And, in addition, Hamann exploited the problem of ignorance esthetically by relating it to Homer, Aristotle, and Shakespeare: "What replaces in Homer the ignorance of those esthetic rules which Aristotle later invented, and what replaces in Shakespeare the ignorance or infringement of those critical laws? Genius is the unanimous answer."[3] What Hamann is saying here is that great men are not great because of their knowledge, but because they are in the hands of a guiding genius which leads them on without the encumbrance of human reason.

In no way can Hamann be called a gifted writer or a consummate artist. His thoughts outraced his pen, and the result was a style overladen with metaphors, interlaced with dialect and foreign quotations, and poured forth in a fragmentary manner. But these sibylline outbursts contained revolutionary, infectious ideas which had a profound influence on the "Stürmer und Dränger," particularly Herder. To his compatriot Hamann Herder owed his acquaintance with English literature—especially with Ossian and Shakespeare—and with Hamann's aid he succeeded in obtaining a position at the Cathedral School in Riga. In the third year of Herder's residence in Riga, his *Fragmente über die neuere deutsche Literatur* (1766–67) were published. The germs of many of Herder's chief opinions are to be found in these *Fragmente*. For instance, his ideas on language, on the relation of German to other literatures, and on the nature of the *Volkslied* all appear here in embryonic form. Like Hamann, he developed a dislike for the cold rationalism of the Enlightenment and stressed the creative freedom of the individual, the primacy of the intuitive senses and passions, and the inner kinship of the soul, language, and poetry of the folk. According to the *Fragmente*, the poetry of the *Volk* is the original, genuine expression of a people and as such preferred over the writings of an overly cultivated civilization. Following this train of thought, a true culture is individualistic and nationalistic, and likewise every original poet must be a nationalistic author. Furthermore, genius is nature which exists beyond the confines of contemporary society.

The restless, dissatisfied young Herder followed a compulsive desire to break out of his provincial shell in order to see more of life; and in the summer of 1769 he left by sea for Nantes and spent nearly five months in France. His stay in that country heightened his revulsion against modern Rationalistic civiliza-

tion, which he likened to a senile person. At the close of his
visit to France, he was appointed traveling tutor to the son of
the prince-bishop of Lübeck; but this appointment came to an
end hardly a year later in Strassburg, where Herder arrived with
his pupil in September, 1770. Relieved of his duties, he took the
opportunity of placing himself in the hands of an eye specialist
in order to cure a recurring malady.

The winter which Herder spent in Strassburg (1770–71) was
of the greatest significance, for it was at this time that the Storm
and Stress movement was born. During the course of a very few
weeks, Goethe sat at Herder's feet as a disciple and learned of
the new revolution in poetics, which Goethe was subsequently
destined to lead. Herder's ideas at this time are best expressed in
what may be regarded as the manifesto of the Storm and Stress,
Von deutscher Art und Kunst. In this collection, edited jointly by
Herder and Goethe, two essays written by Herder himself—
*Auszug aus einem Briefwechsel über Ossian und die Lieder alter
Völker* and *Shakespeare*—proceed in the same vein as the *Fragmente*, although they have a more crystallized form. Writing
about the folk song in general in the "Ossian" essay, Herder says
that the more uninhibited and the more freely active a people
is, the more sensuous, freer, and fuller of lyrical action must be
its poetry. The further away from artificial, scholastic modes of
thought, speech, and writing a people is, the less chance its
songs will become dead literature. The essence and purpose of
these songs depends solely on the lyrical, living, on the as it
were dance-like character of song, on the unity of content and
feeling.

It is by virtue of Herder's insistence that subjective, emotional feeling is the true basis of all artistic creativity that he
caused a re-evaluation of poetry. Herder pointed out to the
young Goethe the great chasm which existed between a simple
song born of heart and feeling and a polished though trivial
Rococo poem of the German Anacreontics. And this fine sensitivity for poetic orginality and genuine content soon made itself
manifest in Goethe's poetry of the Strassburg period.

The theoretical importance of the Ossian essay lies in Herder's
search for the true relationship between art and experience. He
postulates that nature and form are molded by the specific character of a society, which in like manner constitutes and shapes

the experience of the individual writer. Herder concludes, therefore, that poetic form must change according to the nature of experience. By way of illustration he says that the ancient Germanic poetry is as artistic as the Greek or Roman and that the seemingly crude form of the former is the result of a different cultural background.

Herder's second essay, entitled *Shakespeare,* is naturally concerned with the dramatic rather than the lyrical element, but treats its theme in the same manner as above, showing the dependence of dramatic form on the changing nature of man and society. After giving a somewhat impressionistic survey of Shakespeare's age and environment, he argues that a Shakespearean drama must be interpreted as an expression of this specific environment and the spirit of the time; that, seen from this angle, a Shakespearean drama is just as great as a Sophoclean one:

The drama arose in Greece as it could not have in the North. In the North, therefore, it is not and cannot be what it was in Greece. Sophocles' drama and Shakespeare's drama are two things which in a certain sense scarcely have the name in common.[4]

It follows, therefore, that a drama can no longer be judged by the rules of Aristotle, as the pseudo-French Classicists and even Lessing would have one do, but rather by a congenial, sensitive feeling for a poet's and country's own soul.

Herder sees the greatness of Shakespeare in his naturalness. In his characteristic rhapsodic style, Herder praises Shakespeare as a primitive poet endowed with divine power, as a kinsman of the writers of folk songs. Shakespeare is the genius who sheds the garments of civilization, experiences nature directly, and transmits it in its pure form to his audience. This conception of the English poet was certainly incorrect and ephemeral, but it did help to create a Shakespeare mania which persisted until the time of Grabbe. Herder failed to grasp the essence of Shakespeare's tragic power when he supposed all his plays to be dramatized history in the manner of a vast panorama. However, he came closer to the mark when he envisioned the Shakespearean drama as an organism permeated by a world soul, as a single cosmic event created out of the most disparate complexity and out of seeming irrelevancies of plot; and when he recognized Shakespeare's ability to mold a person of paradoxical complexity into a being who is both convincing and eternally human. This approach to Shakespeare, which was novel at the time, was to have a formative effect on Goethe and Lenz and, indirectly, on twentieth-century dramatists.

Herder's *Von deutscher Art und Kunst* is a milestone in German literature. Along with imparting a sense of national identity and an awareness of historical processes, it asserted the value of naturalness and championed genius as that irrational, creative quality which achieves naturalness. Although it was rich in ideas and served as a spiritual force and intellectual spearhead, it is not a work of art. Written in an enthusiastic but fragmentary manner, it lacks form, for Herder lacked the genius he praised so highly. Aware of his own shortcomings, he was quick to impart his thoughts to one whom he recognized as blessed with the genius of poetic creativity, Goethe. But before we focus on Goethe's vital contribution to the Storm and Stress, it will be advantageous, in painting the background of the period, to direct our attention specifically to the genre of the drama. The drama is the particular object of our investigation, and it is the art form which the young geniuses of 1770 admired above all else.

III   The Drama Before 1770

Prior to 1770, the leading critic and dramatist in Germany was Gotthold Ephraim Lessing, who exerted a tremendous influence on the future of German drama by leading the struggle for emancipation from French Neo-Classicism. In fighting against subservience to a standardized French regularity, to "good taste" and stylized formality, Lessing and his colleagues were actually engaged in the struggle of the rising middle class against courtly and court-dominated society. Committed to the idea of reforming German literature by actual example, in addition to his critical efforts, Lessing wrote *Miss Sara Sampson*. It was the first serious German drama since the Renaissance which took its material from the actual life of the middle classes. No longer patterned after French works but after dramas by the Englishman Lillo, *Miss Sara Sampson* deals with average individuals and their fates. The introduction of middle-class heroes was, therefore, a decisive innovation, which was adopted by subsequent German dramatists, including those of the Storm and Stress.

Lessing's antagonism to the French was not directed primarily toward content but toward the form of the drama. Although he still regarded the word of Aristotle as law, Lessing felt that the French had misinterpreted the Poetics, particularly with regard to the three unities. Arguing that rules which pertained to Greek times should not be followed slavishly, Lessing held that the French conception of the unities of time and place was too superficial. The only unity that mattered was that of action, which was vitally related to the unity of dramatic character. Lessing pointed to Shakespeare as a deeper source of inspiration and as a poet more compatible with the German temperament. Shakespeare's dramas exemplified continuous action built around a given character, and his dramatic method demanded free treatment of time and place. In their defiance of all rules, the Storm and Stress dramatists applauded Lessing's disregard of the unities, and, paradoxical as it may seem, *Emilia Galotti,* in spite of its logical structure and compact lucidity, served as a model to men like Gerstenberg, Klinger, and Leisewitz. But, for the most part, the cool rationality of Lessing's style and thinking repelled the young geniuses, who were bent on invoking feeling rather than reason.

The first drama of any consequence which created an atmosphere of highly charged emotional feeling and, in this respect, corresponded to the esthetics of the Storm and Stress, was Gerstenberg's *Ugolino.* Heinrich Wilhelm von Gerstenberg, a German in Danish military service, was born in 1737 and was therefore, at least ten years older than the geniuses of the 1770's. His works form a bridge between the drama of Rationalism and that of the Storm and Stress. It was in the field of literary criticism that Gerstenberg first exerted a significant influence by stimulating Herder and Goethe through his enthusiasm for Shakespeare and for Nordic poetry. In his *Schleswigsche Literaturbriefe* (1766–70) is to be found the best appreciation of Shakespeare that had yet appeared on the Continent. Rejecting Lessing's comparison of Shakespeare to the old Greek models, Gerstenberg admits that both types of drama have some elements in common, but that Shakespeare is not primarily interested in creating "Furcht und Mitleid" and the subsequent tragic catharsis, as were the Greeks. Rather, he aims at a masterful portrayal of men and the world, at a psychological portrait which is effective through its totality. In his effort to achieve a synthesis, and to imitate nature, Gerstenberg argues, Shakespeare justly disregards the unities of time and place. It is fresh thinking of this type which impressed Herder.

A thread running through the *Schleswigsche Literaturbriefe* is the idea of the indispensability of genius for the creation of works of art, and the promotion of Shakespeare as the perfect genius, uniting originality, feeling, divine inspiration, and the creative power of fantasy to form true art. Gerstenberg appreciates Shakespeare's power of expression and his ability to transmit meaning by the accent and melody of speech; yet his main interest lies in Shakespeare's success in conveying violent passion and intense emotion. For him emotion must, at all times, be supercharged in order to make drama effective.

It is this feverish intensity of feeling that Gerstenberg strives for in his tragedy *Ugolino*, published in 1768. The story itself, taken from an episode in Dante's *Inferno*, relates the tragic end of Ugolino and his three sons, who have been condemned to die of hunger in an old tower in Pisa in which they have been imprisoned. The theme demands the greatest concentration of time, place, and action. Throughout all five acts, we see before us a dilapidated tower racked by storm winds, as a consequence of which the author automatically observes the unity of place. The course of the action simply demands one particular stage setting. In fact, the restricted, Kafkaesque location contributes to the inner dynamics of the play, because the poet allows a paranoiac fear of death to break out among the prisoners after an abortive attempt at escape.

Just as the unity of place in this play seems perfectly natural to us, so does the unity of time. Except for a minimum of exposition, all the action transpires in a single night, for Gerstenberg wants to portray the emotional nature of Ugolino and his sons just as their physical and psychical sufferings approach the catastrophic stage. In order to pay lip service to the Aristotelian tenet that a dramatic hero must atone for the tragic guilt he has incurred, Gerstenberg has Ugolino step out of character and accept his fate stoically. He realizes that he has sinned against the government of Pisa, even though he is innocent of wrongdoing toward his avowed enemy, the bishop. To the extent that Ugolino is tried and convicted under false pretenses by the bishop, he is, however, a precursor of those tragic protagonists of the Storm and Stress, who suffer unjustly from tyrannical despotism. In concluding this brief synopsis of the plot, we must mention, for the sake of completeness, the unity of action. We follow the fate of a father and his three sons, who constitute the entire cast.

From the standpoint of its adherence to Aristotelian principles and to its strict economy of form, *Ugolino* points backward to French Classical tragedy. In almost all other aspects, however, it is a forerunner of the Storm and Stress drama. The unrestrained outbursts of anger and vengeance, the fervent pleadings and utter despair—all expressed in exaggerated hyperboles and unrelieved pathos—point to a new style. It was the highly emotional level that is maintained throughout the drama that appealed to the geniuses of the 1770's.

To make a scene all the more vivid Gerstenberg at times resorted to a crudeness which has a downright repulsive effect. In the fifth act, the son, Anselmo, pushed beyond the brink, gnaws at the breasts of his dead mother in the coffin. Such a deviation reminds us of Shakespeare's *Titus Andronicus* and certain sensational baroque tragedies. As we shall see later, Klinger also is guilty of such aberrations in his early dramas, and in the twentieth century it is the Expressionists who often continue this practice of supplying gory detail. In their desire for ecstatic expression, the writers of the Storm and Stress welcomed Gerstenberg's seeming crudities, therefore, as a vehicle of their own emotional needs. Indeed, the entire atmosphere of *Ugolino*, with its unrelieved monotony of gloom and anguish, touched a kindred nerve. Gerstenberg seems to have spent himself in the one drama. Nothing of any import issued from his pen after *Ugolino*, but it and Goethe's *Götz von Berlichingen* were the two dramas that had the greatest impact on the genre in this revolutionary period.

IV   *Goethe, the Spiritual Leader*

Let us return to Goethe in Strassburg, for it was here, and with Goethe as an inspiration and example, that the Storm and Stress was launched in 1770. In the present series of monographs, one

volume is exclusively devoted to Goethe. However, the Storm
and Stress cannot be understood without Goethe, and the dramatists discussed in this book are so utterly dependent on him
that it is necessary to briefly mention his place in the revolutionary literary movement.

At his father's behest, Goethe came to Strassburg in April,
1770, to continue the study of law which he had begun in Leipzig but was forced to interrupt when illness made it necessary
for him to return to Frankfurt. Completely recovered and
anxious for new surroundings, he arrived in Strassburg as a
twenty-two-year-old student. In the fall of 1770 he made the
acquaintance of Johann Gottfried Herder who was to have the
most profound influence on him. Only five years older but already a man of acknowledged intellectual stature, Herder helped
to emancipate Goethe from his Rococo-oriented background by
pointing the way to artistic freedom and spontaneity. Interpret-
ing the doctrines of Rousseau, Herder instilled in him an enthusiasm for the countryside and its inhabitants and for the
genuine, primitive songs of the people. In the manner of Rousseau he seriously questioned the superiority of the eighteenth
century and the Rationalistic doctrine of perfectibility, by contrasting the contemporary age with the Germanic Middle Ages
and the hoary beginnings of civilization.

Herder instilled in Goethe a love for the divine and unadulterated beginnings of civilization, an atmosphere best preserved
in the eighteenth century by the young and the simple country
folk. Goethe was not long in putting the new doctrine into practice when, on an excursion by horseback in October, 1770, to the
idyllic village of Sesenheim, he met and fell in love with Friederike Brion, the sixteen-year-old daughter of the local pastor.
Captivated by her naïve charm and amiable disposition, he
loved and suffered, felt ecstatic joy and heartrending sadness. It
was natural that the young Goethe should take to heart Herder's
ideas of true literature as the expression of a poet's experience,
and of personal feeling as the basis of artistic activity. Thus blos-
somed forth the "Sesenheim Lieder," which struck a new and
pure note in German poetry and freed the lyric from the formal-
ism of the baroque. The love affair between the patrician son of
Frankfurt and the simple village maiden of Sesenheim was destined to be a fleeting one, but the genuine sense of guilt caused

by it and its termination left its mark on the young Goethe and became the inspiration for characters in *Götz von Berlichingen, Werther,* and *Faust.*

How quickly Herder's ideas took root in the mind of Goethe can likewise be seen in the latter's essay *Von deutscher Baukunst,* published in 1773. If the mentor had directed his young protégé's attention to primitive Germanic poetry and to Homer, Ossian, and Shakespeare, the pupil now directed this enthusiasm for genuine, unadulterated art to Erwin von Steinbach, the builder of the Strassburg Minster. It does not matter that many of Goethe's assertions in the essay are highly debatable and even false (such as his concept of Gothic architecture being a specifically German art); the important fact is that a new concept of art subscribing to the temperament of genius emerges. In an emotional, dithyrambic style Goethe rhapsodizes about the creative force of feeling and of heart rather than of cold reason. The essay also champions true art as being characteristic art:

The only true art is characteristic art. If it arises from deep, harmonious, independent feeling, from feeling peculiar to itself; oblivious, yes, ignorant of everything foreign, then it is whole and living, whether it be born from crude savagery or cultured sentiment.[5]

For Goethe each work of art is, then, unique in its origin, setting, and form. It is the duty of the artist to feel the specific individuality of each experience and to give it shape with the help of his God-given genius. These theories, evolved in *Von deutscher Baukunst,* had a formative effect on the Storm and Stress writers, particularly on Lenz and Wagner. Another essay of the same period, *Zum Shakespeares Tag,* also wielded considerable influence. Continuing the deification of Shakespeare inaugurated by Hamann, Herder, and Gerstenberg, Goethe calls the English writer a titanic genius who molds rebellious, unpredictable nature into a harmonious whole.

Goethe's preoccupation with Shakespeare and the Germanic past in 1770 and 1771 culminated in the writing his first completed drama, *Götz von Berlichingen.* Götz is a model hero of the Storm and Stress. As the medieval knight who is the last representative of a healthy, unspoiled, natural community, he fights against the approaching era with its social artificiality and moral corruptness. He sympathizes with the rebellious peasants and at one time even seeks refuge with social outcasts, the gypsies. Freedom is what he wants at all costs. The young generation saw in Götz the inspiration for their fight against an overly refined Rococo culture and a debility which they discerned in their age. The language of *Götz* is forceful, earthy, and masculine. With its fragmentary sentences, coarse epithets, and emotional outbursts, it was to have a powerful influence on the style of the young dramatists who worshiped at Goethe's feet. The character of Götz himself became the model for one of the two basic Storm and Stress types. He was, naturally, the prototype of the vigorous man of action who expresses himself through brave and noble deeds. Trusting his heart and his conscience alone, he believes in spontaneity and natural law and becomes the voice and conscience of the simple people.

In Götz Goethe depicts a historical personage, but at the same time mirrors his own intimate and personal experiences. Like the main character, he is the pure idealist and unbridled individualist who is politically, socially, and intellectually out of tune with his time; but like Weislingen, too, he is irresolute in character and fickle in love. Lenz, Klinger, and Wagner were to follow Goethe's example and use their personal experiences and emotions creatively. In *Götz* the influence of Shakespeare is all-pervading. The young Goethe does not bother about time and locality; his shifts of scene are even more numerous than those of Shakespeare. His action is complicated and often confusing, taking place over many years; and a great number of persons are involved. Upon receiving the original version, which violated the unities still more blatantly, Herder said to Goethe: "Shakespeare has completely ruined you."[6] Yet in its epic breadth *Götz* does catch some of the true spirit of Shakespeare. Language, form, action, and character portrayal are fused into a convincing and colorful whole, which brings the society of the later Middle Ages back to life. Götz is a true German knight of the period of Luther, who speaks in the blunt and vigorous language of the time. The simplicity of the relations between him and his wife and his retainers, the virtues of loyalty and independence, are shown as belonging to this bygone age. Lenz and Wagner were especially quick to recognize how inextricably milieu and atmosphere were interwoven with the conduct of the various strata of society.

If Götz inspired one basic Storm and Stress type—the man of action—Werther provided the stimulus for an equally popular, but diametrically different figure—the sensitive, subjective recluse. While *Götz* had drawn for its emotional content on Goethe's Sesenheim experience, *Werther* is a poetic precipitate of his love for Charlotte Buff in Wetzlar. Having earned his degree in Strassburg, Goethe returned to Frankfurt in the summer of 1771 in order to practice law in conformity with his father's wishes. However, he was unable to adjust to his profession and the bourgeois environment, and in a distraught state of mind he complied with his father's wishes to go to the imperial court of Wetzlar. As customary for the young Goethe, life took precedence over law. In the idyllic atmosphere of Wetzlar, with its calm, rural surroundings, he met and fell deeply in love with Lotte Buff, only to discover that she was already engaged to a Mr. Kestner. In the ecstasy and torment of the ill-fated courtship, the novel *Werther* was born. Like one of its spiritual forebears, Rousseau's *La nouvelle Héloïse, Werther* is written in epistolary form, cherishes the primeval mode of life of the peasant, and drips of sentiment. Although Werther thinks continually of Lotte and writes her a letter before he commits suicide, unhappy love is not the main cause of his death. He perishes of complete frustration in a world which does not understand him, hurts him at every turn, and will not allow him to be himself. In his desire to break with all social conventions and live according to the dictates of his own heart, he sees, alas, the gulf between the real and the ideal become wider and wider, until he has to turn away in anger and disgust from a world which will not submit to his desires.

This sensitive, emotional young genius, who suffers passionate fits of indignation at social injustice, inspired the "Stürmer und Dränger," especially Klinger, Leisewitz, and the young Schiller. The latter writers create characters who are caught in a similar conflict between individual and social environment; but their frustrations and maladjustments are often treated positively, because they cultivate and free emotional feeling, the true essence of one's creative personality. To Goethe, however, *Werther* signified the end of subjective sentimentality and the beginning of a search for a more objective basis of existence. It was the necessary vehicle of an asocial, subjective passion that ran its natural course.

The third major work of the young Goethe which was programmatic for the Storm and Stress was the original version of
Faust, commonly known as the *Urfaust.* Even the title of Maler
Müller's fragmentary drama, *Fausts Leben dramatisiert,* suggests
an affinity in theme. Yet Müller's hero lacks the robust individualism of Goethe's counterpart, although he, too, disregards convention and tradition as a matter of principle. It is Goethe's
depiction of student life as a vehicle of social satire which particularly impressed Müller. But the character in Goethe's drama
which made the profoundest impact on the Storm and Stress
writers is Gretchen. As the simple girl who is exploited and
seduced, she is the prototype of several heroines of Wagner,
Lenz, and Müller. The young men of genius, strongly interested
in exposing corrupt and outdated social mores, depicted in vivid
and realistic detail the environment which caused a Gretchen-
type tragedy. Although Goethe's inherent message of social protest provided a number of themes for the drama of the Storm
and Stress, Goethe's true influence is broader and more encom-
passing. The religion of genius, the abandonment to impulse and
passion, the feeling of sublime vitality, which characterize his
early works, set the tone for the literary creations of the young
men who lived in his shadow.

The first of these men to come under Goethe's influence was
J. M. R. Lenz. As a young theological student who had already
published minor literary works, he met Goethe in Strassburg in
1771, and they maintained a close relationship for the next five
years. Talented and impressionable, Lenz was also highly eccentric and imitated and worshiped Goethe to the degree that he
earned the ridicule of his friends. When Goethe allowed his
friendship for Friederike Brion to cool, Lenz began courting her
in Sesenheim. Thwarted in his efforts to win Friederike, he next
turned his attention to Goethe's married sister, Cornelia. In the
meantime, he sought Goethe's advice on essays and plays which
he was writing. As we shall see, Lenz profited much from his
relations with his mentor, but he also suffered greatly from a
feeling of inferiority.

When Goethe left Strassburg for Frankfurt and subsequently
for Wetzlar, only to return again to Frankfurt, his personal con-
tacts widened. Along the way he met men who were not of the
highest literary rank, but nevertheless left their imprint on the

contemporary scene. Among these were the physiognomist Lavater, the poet-philosopher Jacobi, and the author of a popular autobiography, Jung-Stilling. Goethe corresponded with Bürger in Göttingen and with the venerable Klopstock in Hamburg. Although Goethe and the abovementioned literati profited mutually from a lively interchange of ideas, none of these men became disciples of Goethe in the manner of Lenz.

An equally devoted follower of Goethe's was the Storm and Stress dramatist Friedrich Maximilian Klinger. A native of Frankfurt like Goethe, he possessed unbounded energy and obvious talent. Since he was the son of very poor people, Goethe came to his aid and enabled him to study at the University of Giessen. If Lenz corresponds to the Werther type, the image Klinger projected is more like Götz, a heroic superman, or Prometheus. Klinger cultivated a genuine and humble admiration for Goethe, whereas Lenz, having become somewhat paranoid, often imagined himself to be the equal of "the master." It was especially the style and spirit of the young Goethe that Klinger imitated. His dramas reflect the ebullient enthusiasm and unbridled passion of Goethe's Storm and Stress lyrics; his language shows a remarkable kinship to the virile, staccato outbursts of Götz.

Another personal acquaintance of Goethe in his Strassburg and Frankfurt days, and a significant dramatist of the 1770's, was Heinrich Leopold Wagner. He was born in Strassburg, and like Goethe, studied law there; he then practiced in Frankfurt, where he came into closer contact with Goethe, but met an untimely death in 1779 at the age of thirty-two. Compared with Klinger he was not a prolific writer, but his two dramas *Die Reue nach der That* and *Die Kindsmörderin*, are typical Storm and Stress examples of satirical realism, combining intense feeling and a realistic grasp of the outer world. The theme and content of his social satire borrows heavily from Goethe's creations, particularly from *Faust*.

In 1775 still other figures were drawn into Goethe's orbit, among whom were the minor poets, the brothers Christian and Friedrich Leopold, Grafen zu Stolberg. They accompanied Goethe on his trip to Switzerland, were completely taken by him, and were responsible for conveying their enthusiasm for him to the group of poets known as the Göttingen "Hainbund." The work of one of these, Johann Anton Leisewitz, will form an integral part of our study. Another colorful and talented personality, who met Goethe and his inner circle of friends in Frankfurt in 1775, was Friedrich Müller, the painter (usually referred to as Maler Müller). Although he made Mannheim his home, he frequently went to Frankfurt and enjoyed an intimate association with Goethe as well as with Lenz, Klinger, and Wagner. His earlier writings reflect the same sentimental and idyllic atmosphere as Gessner's *Idyllen*, but after 1775 the new influence makes itself felt in language as well as theme. As mentioned before, Müller's *Faust* owes a great debt to Goethe, and his drama of medieval knighthood, *Golo und Genoveva*, shows a spiritual affinity to *Götz*.

Of the five dramatists treated in our study, only one—Leisewitz—had no personal contact with Goethe. Born in Hannover in 1752, he studied at the university of Göttingen, where, through Hölty's intercession, he became a member of the "Hainbund." Of a retiring nature, with morbid and hypochondriac tendencies, he felt at home in the quiet atmosphere of Göttingen. Although his only full-length drama, *Julius von Tarent*, shows a kinship to Lessing's dramas in structure, its characters definitely breathe the air of the Storm and Stress. The protagonist, Julius, is a Werther type, who revels in feeling and sensitive introspection, while his younger brother, Guido, is, like Götz, a man of action and of blunt and vigorous speech. The brothers Stolberg represented the most likely intermediaries between Goethe and Leisewitz, but even without them it was not difficult for an aspiring poet in Göttingen to find access to the young Goethe's works.

The impact of Goethe on the young men in his immediate circle of friends and on those on the periphery of his sphere of influence manifested itself in their amazing productivity. Lenz enjoyed Goethe's favor between 1771 and 1776, and in the course of that period he authored his theory of the drama and all of his important plays. Klinger, stimulated by *Götz*, *Werther*, and *Clavigo*, published six Storm and Stress dramas within the short period of three years (1774–76). In the same period Wagner completed his two main dramas, Maler Müller wrote his *Faust* fragment, and Leisewitz created his *Julius von Tarent*. It is all the more remarkable how all five poets lost the incentive for writing dramas after Goethe left for Weimar. In fact, Klinger was the only member of the group who continued to publish regularly after 1776, though in a different genre and spirit. The flash of genius passed as suddenly as it came.

CHAPTER 2

Lenz: Life of a Genius

IN A WAY it is an indictment of our age that Jacob Michael Reinhold Lenz, whose life and works are a record of a torn, tragic, and unstable personality, should wield such a tremendous influence on German dramatists of the twentieth century. No writer of his time approaches him in pessimism, despair, and irony; no one exhibits a more acute social awareness, nor a profounder insight into the riddle of the human situation itself.

Lenz was born on January 12, 1751, at Sesswegen, in Livonia, a part of the Baltic provinces of Russia which contained a large German-speaking population. His father, Christian David Lenz, had studied theology at the University of Halle, the fountainhead of German Pietism. Determined to establish himself in the Baltic area, he accepted in 1740 a position as "Hofmeister" (tutor). It was customary for young theologians in Livonia to bide their time in this fashion until they obtained a church of their own. After two years, the young tutor embarked on his clerical career which led from pastorates in village churches in Serben, Sesswegen, and Dorpat, to the office of General Superintendent of Livonia. It was in Dorpat that the son, Jakob, spent his formative years, from eight to seventeen. As that of an isolated, provincial town, Dorpat's cultural life was guided mainly by ministers and tutors, and the inhabitants were morally sustained by Pietism. Jakob's father was a tyrannical but deeply religious person who brought up his children in the consciousness of sin and hellfire. In his numerous theological writings, Christian Lenz was an avowed foe of Rationalism and fostered an intimate, personal religion. Following the tenets of Pietism, he believed that the release of one's pent-up emotions was a vital element in experiencing a direct relationship to God. This Pietistic upbringing left its mark on the sensitive and impressionable son, Jakob. From his mother he had inherited a weak, sickly constitution and a delicate temperament inclined to melancholy; from his father a volatile disposition given to violent and passionate outbursts.

At the behest of his father, young Lenz matriculated in 1768 at the University of Königsberg as a student of theology. Although he attended the theological lectures of Lilienthal and Reccard, the only professor who made a distinct impression on him was Immanuel Kant. A rather stilted Sapphic ode, written in Kant's honor, testifies to the esteem in which Lenz held his mentor. Strangely enough, it was not Kant's philosophic system which influenced the young student, but rather the philosopher's enthusiasm for Rousseau and his precept that all human knowledge and endeavor should be subject to the most careful analysis and criticism. Besides Kant, Hamann, who was known as the "Magus im Norden," lived in Königsberg at this time. We do not know if they were close friends, but they subsequently carried on a correspondence, and it may be reasonably assumed that Lenz was acquainted with Hamann's writings.

There is no question but that Lenz was early obsessed by the urge to write creatively. His first poems, dating back to his years in Dorpat, ape Klopstock in form and theme and exude the sentiment and heaven-scaling enthusiasm of the latter's *Messias*. An early attempt at writing drama, *Der verwundete Bräutigam,* likewise appeals to the emotions for its effect. Feeling and declamation compensate for a lack of action and an inherent weakness in character portrayal. The play, borrowing heavily from the sentimental French comedy in vogue at the time, gives no inkling of the dramatic creations which were to follow a decade later. A longer descriptive poem, *Die Landplagen,* is of interest not because it imitates the style of Klopstock, but because Lenz treats personal experiences realistically. Equally noteworthy is the sign of an English influence, for the poem obviously shows similarities to Thomson's *Seasons* and Young's *Night Thoughts.* With reference to the latter poem, it is not yet the inherent message of genius which inspires Lenz, but rather the veneration of genuine, unadulterated nature and of unaffected simplicity.

The translation of Shakespeare's *Love's Labour's Lost,* which Lenz began in Königsberg, bears testimony to his continuing interest in English literature and to his ability as a linguist. In fact, Lenz gave English and French lessons as a tutor in the home of a nobleman of Königsberg, and his knowledge of foreign languages led indirectly to his leaving the Königsberg area, for when two Baltic barons, the brothers von Kleist, asked Lenz to accompany them to France as an interpreter and travel companion, he agreed. Quite rashly and without parental approval, he left the university in the spring of 1771, only one semester before his final examinations.

On the journey to Strassburg, the party stopped off in Berlin and Leipzig, whose student life sufficiently impressed Lenz to be alluded to in *Der Hofmeister*. Since the von Kleist brothers had come to France to join the French army and their regiment was stationed in the Alsatian area, Lenz soon became acquainted with the countryside and the seamy side of garrison life. His rather torturous experiences in army billets were compensated, however, by the intellectual companionship he found at a daily dinner group in Strassburg presided over by a bachelor lawyer Salzmann. In this circle, the bright young men of Strassburg discussed culture in general and literature in particular, and it here that the cult of genius, known later as the Storm and Stress, first came into being. Herder exerted the greatest influence in the formative days of the group, but when he left in the spring of 1771, Goethe became the leader.

A new world suddenly opened up for Lenz. Throwing overboard the ballast he had accumulated in his Königsberg days, he was avid to learn the new message of Homer, Ossian, Shakespeare, and Young. The worship of nature cultivated by his new companions enhanced his natural inclination for the realistic, and their passion for drama and the theater was to have an indelible effect on him. He immediately was drawn to Goethe's genius and had the compulsive desire not only to write literature equal to that of his idol but to fall in love with Goethe's women. Though he was unhappy enough never to win love in return, he loved Friederike Brion after Goethe's departure and formed an emotional attachment to Goethe's sister, Cornelia, who was married and lived in the neighborhood of Strassburg. In his neurotic state of mind, he craved women outside of Goethe's sphere as well. The only prerequisite seems to have been that each new lady friend was already linked with a man either in a clandestine way or through engagement or marriage. Thus he had an obsession for Cleophe Fibich, the commoner paramour of the elder Kleist; and a little later he fell hopelessly in love with Henriette von Waldner, a lady of the aristocracy about to marry a nobleman.

This strange desire to possess another man's woman and to write better than the acknowledged genius, Goethe, points to a peculiar quirk in Lenz's nature. It is understandable that he suffered and experienced a maximum of torment in his situation; but that he seemed to revel in misfortune and considered it his way of life makes one suspect aberrations in his personality. In a letter to Lavater he admits that his greatest sufferings were caused by his own heart, but that the most unbearable condition would be one in which he were free of all suffering.[1] And to Sophie von La Roche he writes that ever since his childhood he had been destined to run his head against a wall.[2] Moods of despair and joy, irony and illusion, satire and reverence alternately seized him, driving him to excess and caricature. Though he was a puckish and affectionate character, he also possessed a streak of malice which alienated and wounded his friends. His unstable and fickle nature generated qualities often associated with adolescence. But Lenz really never grew up.

That Lenz should find it difficult to select a profession is not hard to believe. Without sounding convincing, he confides to Salzmann that he has decided on law, because theology no longer fulfills his aspirations.[3] Although Lenz felt no vocation for the Church, he enjoyed theological discussions, and many of his essays from the Strassburg period deal with theological issues. What is disconcerting, however, is that a man for whom life was an irreconcilable nightmare should have retained the Pietist sense of sin and the Rationalistic concepts of perfectibility and happiness.

In 1774 Lenz severed his relations with the Kleists, but continued his studies in Strassburg, eking out a meager existence from the honoraria of his writings and from tutorial fees. What seems to have sustained him in this difficult period was his friendship with Goethe. Even though Goethe was now in Weimar, he visited Lenz in Strassburg in the spring of 1775 on the way to Switzerland and again on his return. Together they took long walks in Strassburg and the surrounding countryside and called on Goethe's sister, Cornelia, and her new husband, Schlosser, who lived in nearby Emmendingen. Goethe and Lenz carried on a regular and mutually stimulating correspondence from June, 1773 until the spring of 1776, but the early part of 1775 represented the height of their relationship and of Lenz's fanatical veneration of Goethe. The two young men exchanged first drafts of manuscripts, Lenz sending Goethe, for his advice and comment, the early versions of all his major works: *Der Hofmeister, Der neue Menoza, Die Soldaten, Anmerkungen übers Theater,* and the imitations of Plautus.

The last two years in Strassburg (1774–76) was the period during which Lenz enjoyed the highest esteem among the literati of Germany. Sophie la Roche regarded him with favor. Hamann, Lavater, Herder, Zimmermann, Merck, and Boie carried on active correspondence with him. He became acquainted with the Prince of Weimar and Knebel, and the brothers Stolberg sought out his company. In newspapers he was mentioned along with Goethe as the second German Shakespeare.[4] In Strassburg, Lenz filled the intellectual vacuum caused by Goethe's departure by founding a society called "Deutsche Gesellschaft in Strassburg" and functioning as its guiding spirit. Numbering among its members Leopold Wagner—one of the subjects of our study—leading professors and diplomats, Schlosser, and two French men of letters, the society was patriotic in outlook and fostered German culture in the broadest sense of the word. *Der Bürgerfreund,* a periodical which was sponsored by the society and functioned for two years, contained a variety of articles by miscellaneous authors, but those by Lenz are of more concern to us since they reveal his diverse interests and talents. Contributions by Lenz include essays on the Alsatian dialect and on the language of the lower classes, a critique of Shakespeare's frequent scene changes, comments on an old English ballad, a defense of Goethe's *Werther,* and some poems of his own.

It seems ironical that Lenz, who enjoyed the respect of Goethe and the leading men of letters of his day, could not adjust to reality. His relationship with the world and his fellow men remained an unhappy one, and once more, a disappointing love affair provided the impetus for causing an imbalance. Upon learning that the aforementioned Henriette von Waldner had become engaged to another man, he despaired of life and contemplated suicide. The passion for her was all the more grotesque since he knew her only through letters. There were other factors which made a further stay in Strassburg intolerable. He had fallen into debt, had no prospect of earning a livelihood, and enjoyed less and less rapport with his immediate circle of acquaintances.

Writing still offered solace, and Lenz's chief works which stem from this period—the tragicomedies *Der Hofmeister* and *Die Soldaten* and the novel fragment *Der Waldbruder*—do not merely express a Storm and Stress attempt to overcome the monotony of the classical art through a diversity approximating life in the raw; rather, in the dramatic utilization of the inconsistent and the ludicrous the poet was able to unburden himself of the torment of emotional discrepancies within himself. The latter were caused, in part, by a clash between Lenz's unbridled fantasy and the basic contradictions it occasioned, as well as by a tension stemming from his inveterate tendency to vacillate between self-aggrandizement and servile self-abasement. Thus Lenz, pridefully aware of the problematics of his inner life, loved to portray shocking and bizarre elements in his works. The disintegration of the external form of his plays into a loose, episodic structure, as well as his characters' tendency to lose their composure at a critical moment, supply further evidence of Lenz's effort to find emotional release in his writings.

With his back against the wall, and determined to leave Strassburg at all costs, Lenz entertained the idea of going to America to fight in the Revolution, only to decide, at the last minute, to follow Goethe to Weimar. On the way to Weimar, he spent several days in Darmstadt as the guest of Merck, and in Frankfurt Klinger and Schleiermacher greeted him, appearing in full Werther costume—blue coat, yellow vest, and white hat with yellow trim. Clearly in these regalia they recognized a member in full standing of the cult of genius. Lenz stayed at the home of Goethe's parents and also met Wagner, whom he knew from his Strassburg days.

Arriving in Weimar with high hopes on April 4, 1776, Lenz looked forward to a renewed association with Goethe and also with the Duke of Weimar, whom he presented with a fantastic project for the reform of his army. But impulsive, rash, quick-tempered, and unaccustomed to court etiquette as he was, he soon fell out of favor, and by June he had removed to Berka, a quiet little village in the Thuringian forest several hours distant from Weimar. Here *Tantalus*, a satirical, dramatic poem about life in Weimar, originated and still won Goethe's approval. A novel fragment, *Der Waldbruder*, written at the same time, was the cause of increased friction between the two men, because it portrayed Goethe as an Epicurean and egotist.

Lenz increasingly resented Goethe's social success, and some statement on Lenz's part, either written or oral, relative to Goethe's relation to Frau von Stein, led to a final rift between the two poets. Goethe merely writes in his diary for November 26 "Lenzens Eseley,"[5] and no longer able to tolerate the erratic genius, he was primarily responsible for Lenz's leaving the Weimar area permanently on December 1. Although petty strifes triggered the disassociation of the two men, their differences were more fundamental. In Weimar Goethe had outgrown the Storm and Stress eccentricities of the Strassburg era and had matured into a responsible individual who could view life and his literary creations more objectively. Lenz, on the other hand, was still a creature of impulse, a pawn of his emotions, and lacked the capacity to grow up. Though Lenz alternatingly worshiped and hated Goethe, the latter had been his port in a storm and his literary inspiration; and when Goethe severed relations, the affects on his protégé were catastrophic. Lenz lost hold of himself; and no literary work of any significance was to issue henceforth from his pen.

Virtually expelled from Weimar, Lenz retraced his steps to Alsace, was the penniless guest of Schlosser, Goethe's brother-in-law, visited Lavater, spent well over six months in aimless wandering through Switzerland, and in November, 1777, suffered a first attack of madness. Tormented by hallucinations and a feeling of guilt, he committed one preposterous act after another; and in the village of Fouday, Switzerland, he even attempted to raise a girl by the name of Friederike from the dead. During Lenz's period of derangement, Schlosser seems to have expressed the most genuine concern for him, and it was Schlosser's intercession which induced Lenz's brother to bring him home. On July 23, 1779, he arrived by ship in Riga after an eleven-year absence. Lenz recovered his sanity—at least for a while—and went to Saint Petersburg and Moscow in search of congenial surroundings and a livelihood. He functioned sporadically as a tutor and teacher and even tried to write plays of which several fragments have been preserved. But, broken in body and spirit, he spent his last years in misery and was picked up dead in a Moscow street on the night of May 24, 1792.

The uncertainty of his future, his unsuccessful attempts at love, and his inability to compete with Goethe helped convince Lenz that his life was a failure. Kindermann refers to his diary as the history of a pathological passion.[6] His view of existence as being basically incongruous has a curiously modern ring, and his dramatic art, which is a compensation for his inner futility, reflects a dramatist of genius far in advance of his time. His erratically brilliant plays, which express a social protest and convey an ironic sense of futility, anticipate the message of the mid-twentieth-century dramatist. The episodic, disjointed form of Lenz's dramas serve, as well, as a vehicle eminently suited for the portrayal of the modern Weltanschauung.

I Anmerkungen übers Theater

Lenz developed his radical concept of episodic drama in his *Anmerkungen übers Theater*, which appeared in 1774 and is his only theoretical work. Along with Herder's *Shakespeare*, Goethe's *Zum Shakespears Tag*, and Mercier's *Nouvel Essai sur le théâtre*, it forms the dramaturgy of the Storm and Stress. Lenz tells us that his *Anmerkungen* were written before the appearance of the Herder-Goethe collection *Von deutscher Art und Kunst* and befor the publication of *Götz*. This is possible, but at the same time it may be assumed that Lenz at least knew something about the spirit of Herder's and Goethe's essays before their publication. As we have noted, Lenz was well acquainted with Goethe and his literary group in Strassburg, and his sudden interest in drama and in Shakespeare owed much to the new environment. The disjointed, unsystematic form of the *Anmerkungen* can be attributed, in part, to their origin. The essay was delivered initially as a rashly prepared lecture before the local literary society, but eventually several independent essays were added or inserted; after the appearance of *Götz* and *Von deutscher Art und Kunst*, Lenz's theoretical study was once more scrutinized and superficially edited. The rhapsodic outbursts and flights of fancy which permeate it reveal the influence of Hamann and Herder and also the mercurial spirit of the author.

In attacking the French pseudo-Classical theater and championing Shakespeare, Lenz continued where Lessing and Mercier left off. But when Lenz throws overboard the Aristotelian tenets, which Lessing considered a norm, he shows his true colors as a member of the Storm and Stress movement. Echoing the sentiments of Goethe's *Zum Shakespears Tag*, Lenz asserts that Greek drama was originally an important part of religious worship, produced specifically for Greeks, so that the imitation of Greek drama in the eighteenth century cannot be more than a parody. The Greeks believed in the terrible power of fate, which determined the destiny of man.[7] This outlook is evident in plays built around the inscrutable and arbitrary actions of a higher power that cannot be questioned, with the result that the conduct of a Greek tragic hero is not in keeping with his basic motives. Lenz considers such a concept of action outmoded and unsuitable for modern, Christian times;[8] and out of date as well is the rigid dramatic form which evolved from the fatalistic Weltanschauung of the Greeks.

Unity of action, for example, which depicted the deterministic course of events as dictated from above, was logical and all-important for the Greeks; and as a corollary, the story, or the action of the play, was more important to them than the characters. But Lenz argues—as did Mercier before him—that for modern man exactly the reverse is true. Portrayal of an individual is all-important; as he says: "The chief feeling in a tragedy is the character which creates its events."[9] According to Lenz, a character is propelled from within, and he alone is the key to his fate. However, a man is a very complex being, and it is the task of the artist of genius to depict all the facets of a personality, which can best be accomplished by a multiplicity of actions and events rather than by a single unified action. In this connection Lenz states that

the variety of characters and psychologies is nature's storehouse; here alone the divining rod of genius is able to locate the treasure. And nature alone determines the infinite variety of actions and events in the world.[10]

Lenz furnishes detailed instructions as to how this multiplicity of action and place in a modern drama should be staged:

In our case it is a series of actions which follow each other like thunderbolts, the one supporting and illuminating the other, until they merge into a magnificent whole, whose purpose is no more and no less to . . . reveal the main character.[11]

Short scenes are to follow one another in a rapid sequence,
which, in turn, serve to narrate a sequence of events. It is obvious that the dramatic structure which Lenz advocates introduces
an epic quality into the drama, and a major biographer of Lenz,
M. N. Rosanow, wrote at the outset of the twentieth century that
Lenz was unable to distinguish between the epic and the dramatic and mixed the two forms. [12] But in the present day we
would say that Lenz's theory, put into practice in *Der Hofmeister*
and *Die Soldaten,* anticipates the episodic structure of the
drama so much in vogue since Brecht.

As expressed in the quotation above, the multiplicity of scenes
and actions is not a haphazard innovation but serves a definite
purpose, that of revealing the characteristic individuality of a
personage. Finding fault with the French Classical dramatists
for portraying dull, stereotyped figures on the stage, Lenz demands characters that are typical, genuine, and true to life:

According to my feeling, I appreciate the characteristic, even the
caricature, ten times more than the ideal, speaking hyperbolically;
for it is ten times harder to depict a figure with the accuracy and
truth with which a genius recognizes it than to labor for ten years at
an ideal of beauty which, in the final analysis, is only such in the
brain of the artist who created it.[13]

When Lenz asserts that the characteristic is preferable to the
ideal and the beautiful, he is breaking not only with the French
Classicists but with Aristotle himself and anticipating a twentieth-century attitude.

Of the three unities Lenz criticizes primarily that of action;
but in advocating a loose, episodic structure he necessarily dis-
cards also the unities of time and place. By calling unity of place
the unity of the chorus, he dismisses its *raison d'être,* just as
Lessing had done. Unity of time, Lenz asserts, may justifiably be
limited to a day in certain instances, but if the hero operates
with the ten-year Trojan war as a background, the time span of
the drama must reflect this long duration. In contrast to the
Greeks, Lenz feels that the Germans are not content with a
simple action, a single place, and a limited time; they need color,
individuality, and infinite variety: the movement of a world is

of more import than that of a house.[14] It is the mission of the
poet to re-create a world on a small scale; to synthesize and dis-
til a host of successive experiences into an all-embracing poetic
unity. In the final analysis Lenz wants to imitate nature, just as
the Rationalists professed to do; however, his world of nature
has infinite variety and is not limited to the orderly, beautiful
universe of the dramas of Enlightenment. In professing that a
dramatist should copy nature and not Aristotle, Lenz is seeking
boldy to abandon all rules in the spirit of his predecessors, Young
and Mercier. The latter men presuppose the innate genius of
the poet, which frees him from the burden of literary models,
rules, and authorities.

Is there or has there ever been a dramatist who has written
plays according to the theory spelled out in the *Anmerkungen
übers Theater?* Lenz says that there has been one—Shakespeare.
In comparing Shakespeare's *Julius Caesar* with Voltaire's *Mort
de Cesar*, he selects the character of Brutus to show how the
French version is merely a silhouette or marionette, while Shakespeare's counterpart is a many-sided person portrayed in all his
fullness. Lenz notes that Shakespeare felt free to employ a sequence of actions, for this method enabled him to breathe life
into his protagonists and to achieve unity of character, which is
the only unity that matters. A cardinal point that Lenz makes in
his *Anmerkungen* is that the Aristotelian form of the drama is
too restrictive to encompass the psychological complexities of
human nature, while Shakespeare's structure points the way toward remedying this situation. From Shakespeare, Lenz also de-
rives his definitions for tragedy and comedy. Basing his theory of
tragedy on the study of Shakespeare's so-called dramatic his-
tories, he says that tragedy is built around remarkable individuals; comedy, on the other hand, subordinates characters to happenings.

In 1774, the same year in which the *Anmerkungen* appeared,
the five *Lustspiele nach dem Plautus fürs deutsche Theater* (comedies based on Plautus) were published. Although Lenz's versions are more original and more flexible than the Plautus adap-
tations of Lessing and show his predilection and ability for portraying realistic detail, they do not incorporate the new dramatic
theory as outlined in the *Anmerkungen*. But Lenz's first original
play, *Der Hofmeister*, was to put the new ideas into practice.

II Der Hofmeister

As the title implies, the drama deals with a tutor. In concerning himself with the profession of his protagonist, Lenz is following in the footsteps of Diderot, who would have a dramatist stress, whenever possible, the occupation of his characters. However, Lenz's drama also has a subtitle, *Vorteile der Privaterziehung* ("Advantages of a Private Education"), which turns out to be a spoof, for during the course of the action we never get to see the advantages of this type of education, from the standpoint of either the teacher or the pupil. The irony involved here provides the key to Lenz's creative art. On the one hand, he writes with the zeal of a social reformer; and on the other, he is the cynic who sees through the futility of it all. Labeling Lenz an idealistic cynic will be fruitful in analyzing his plays.

On examining the problem of genre, the question of duality reappears. On the title page, Lenz calls *Der Hofmeister* a "Komödie," while in a letter to Salzmann he speaks of "mein Trauerspiel," when referring to it in its manuscript form.[15] This ambiguity does not resolve itself if we re-examine Lenz's definitions in the *Anmerkungen*. When he states that tragedy is built around colorful individuals, this is certainly true of *Der Hofmeister;* and when a comedy, in Lenz's words, subordinates characters to events, this rule is not violated in the drama. Social and environmental factors receive considerable attention and determine the conduct of the individuals.

Lenz's ambition was to create a new form of the drama, which combined the advantages of tragedy with those of comedy, where scenes of deepest pathos alternate with those of effective comedy. Rosanow,[16] as well as the English critic Garland, feel that Lenz has failed in this endeavor.[17] In a recent study on tragicomedy, Guthke comes to the reverse conclusion, however. Defining tragicomedy as a drama in which the characters are comical figures in a tragic situation and portrayed against a tragic background, Guthke refers to *Der Hofmeister* as an excellent example of this genre.[18] In fact, tragicomedy, illustrated so well by *Der Hofmeister*, is acknowledged as the best art form to effectively express the incongruity of life.

In the first act there is little to suggest that Lenz contemplates a new dramatic form. We are introduced to the principals of the play by means of a traditional exposition: Läuffer, a young man who has just finished his studies at the university and is penniless and in need of employment, has been hired as a private tutor in the home of Major Berg to teach his two children—a boy, who is a spoiled brat, and a girl, Gustchen, who is the delicate daughter of a doting father. The scene is Lenz's boyhood home of Livonia, and the action is based on actual events which the author experienced. By using true-to-life situations and realistic dialogue, Lenz is following the example of Lessing, Mercier, Herder, and Goethe and the theory of the *Anmerkungen,* as opposed to the tradition of the French Classical theater.

Through vital and spontaneous dialogue we get to know the remaining members of the family—the Major's wife; his brother, the Councillor; and the latter's son Fritz, who loves Gustchen. And through the family conversations we gradually surmise what the play is seemingly all about: it discusses and seeks a solution for a basic conflict which has arisen between the nobility and the middle class in matters of a social and pedagogical nature. The German nobility, stubbornly clinging to the prejudices and ceremonial superficialities of its decadent Rococo culture, is exploiting and suppressing the middle class, which it despises and considers inferior. This disturbing state of affairs, crying for reform on a national level, is communicated to us in its vital immediacy in the case of Läuffer versus Berg.

In depicting class foibles and customs, Lenz does not resort to a black-and-white technique; rather, in the spirit of the *Anmerkungen,* aristocrat and burgher are shown to be very complex individuals, possessing good and bad traits, and for an infinite variety of reasons. Lenz employs Councillor Berg as a narrator or commentator to initiate the discussion and presents the facts as objectively as possible; and in using this impassive bystander to inject the author's views, he creates a figure far in advance of his time.

Councillor Berg blames the nobility for not building common schools where the children of all classes could associate and learn mutually to respect each other; instead of this, the nobleman entrusts his children to the care of private tutors, whom he pays poorly and treats like servants. However, the educated young burghers are also reproached for neglecting the welfare of the citizenry; for instead of using their education for the good of the state, they dissipate their talents as tutors for the nobility and thereby lower themselves to the status of domestic servants. With respect to Läuffer, specifically, the Councillor shows little sympathy, for he says that any man so lacking in backbone as to work at tutoring for the aristocracy deserves no better fate.

In line with his theory, outlined earlier, that characters are the cardinal element in the drama, Lenz takes great pains to delineate his dramatis personae, so that they come to life as colorful, genuine, and individualized persons. Councillor Berg, whose views were expounded above, is the wise, tolerant man with enlightened ideas. Free of the prejudices of his class, he chides the aristocracy for abusing its privileges and for neglecting its civic responsibilities. A discerning observer of human nature, he communicates his views frankly and tactfully. The middle class, in the person of Läuffer, likewise receives its share of criticism for being so passive and servile. Filled with the ideas of Rousseau, the Councillor preaches a message of freedom and equality:

Without freedom life goes downhill and backwards. Freedom is the element of man just as water is that of a fish; and a man who renounces freedom poisons the noblest spirit of his blood, nips the sweetest joys of life in the bud and kills himself.[19]

Councillor Berg carries Lenz's banner of social reform, and it is interesting to note that he is the only figure in the drama that is not treated comically.

All the other members of the aristocracy have foibles which make them objects of comic derision. The Major is a blustering tyrant, who is proud, irascible, but overly sentimental, especially when the welfare of his daughter is at stake. He is a descendant of Lessing's Odoardo Galotti. The Major's wife, a colorful representative of the superficial, decadent Rococo age, is a vain coquette, who combines aristocratic arrogance with a disdain for the burgher. True to character, she helps to swindle the tutor out of part of his salary, cares little about his academic qualifications, but is overjoyed that he speaks French, which is, in her eyes, the language of the elite. Graf Wermuth, the admirer and confidant of the Major's wife, exposes himself from the moment we meet him as an aristocratic snob. He knows and cares little about art, but lives the life of a selfish hedonist. Were it not for the Councillor, we might be led to think that Lenz was criticizing the nobility as such. It must be remembered that at this time no one had the audacity to criticize the members of the privileged class as a whole—one only singled out some of their foolish habits which should be corrected.

If the first act, and even the beginning of the second, seem to suggest a unified play of social involvement, this illusion is quickly shattered. Scene and plot change in bewildering fashion, so that by the end of the play we count no fewer than thirty-five scenes and three plots. Led astray by Shakespeare and Goethe's *Götz*, Lenz shifts around so arbitrarily that it is sometimes impossible to fathom how all the actions in progress interrelate. The adventures and perils of Läuffer at first occupy the center of the stage, to be followed by the love affair of Fritz von Berg and Gustchen, caught up in the maelstrom of student life. A third plot, introduced late in the drama, focuses on the romance of Pätus and Jungfer Rehaar, which is foiled, for a time, by the attempted seduction of Miss Rehaar by an amoral aristocrat named von Seiffenblase.

To be sure, a diverse theme of social criticism pervades all the plots, as it points an accusing finger at aristocratic parasitism, middle-class passivity, unwholesome environments for students, class-structured attitudes toward sex, inequalities in teacher's salaries, and a general callous unconcern for one's fellow man. But this is only part of Lenz's message and must even be construed cynically, for Lenz casts serious doubts on man's ability to change. And this is where the confusing, disjointed arrangement of scenes begins to make sense. By using the loose, episodic structure to focus on certain individuals, Lenz attempts to show these characters under the sway of multiple social and economic determinants which dictate their conduct and prevent reform.

Läuffer offers the best illustration of Lenz's philosophy, simply because more episodes are devoted to him than to any other character. In the first act, he appears to be a frivolous academic tramp who has spent too much time in coffee houses and at dances to obtain a solid background in his field. But he blames society for placing him in a hostile world. For financial reasons, his father, a cleric, will not allow him to follow in his footsteps, and the Councillor, who wields power, will not give him a position in the town school. He is forced, for financial reasons, to become a tutor in the home of aristocrats, whom he detests. Soliloquizing as the Councillor and the Major approach, he utters these words:

There he comes with the Major; I don't know why, but I detest him more than the devil. The fellow has something in his face which is unbearable to me. (*Walks past the Councillor and the Major with an obsequious bow*).[20]

Contorting himself into such reassuring servile postures for those who treat him with indifference and contempt, he projects himself as a repellent weakling. Although he is hostile and suspicious, he remains passive toward those who exploit him and is, in the last analysis, a social marionette. Läuffer's character and conduct are reinforced a little later on when he gushes forth with social pleasantries and fawningly kisses the hand of the Major's wife, whom he inwardly detests: "O . . o . . verzeihen Sie dem Entzücken, dem Enthusiasmus, der mich hinreisst. (*Küsst ihr die Hand.*)"[21] ("Oh . . . Oh, excuse the rapture, the feeling which overwhelms me [*kisses her hand*].") Lenz's use of language to suggest gesture prefigures the technique of Grabbe, Büchner, and Brecht. A forerunner in the use of mimetic gesture, Lenz uses such histrionics to make an immediate visual impression and and to communicate to his audience an awareness of the social forces behind the action depicted.

Pantomime and gesture continue to supplement dialogue in the scenes involving Läuffer and his pupil Gustchen. Since Fritz is away at the university, Läuffer fills the void by becoming Gustchen's lover as well as her tutor. Discussing *La nouvelle Héloise* and calling each other "Romeo" and "Julie," the two lovers reflect the latest cultural fads. In Lenz's highly class-structured society, in which interclass marriages never occur and characters never transcend their mores, Läuffer's and Gustchen's relationship is a strange one. But here again social and even instinctual determinants provide the key to their behavior. Does not Läuffer succumb to physical lust because he has lost his self-esteem in his servile position in the house of the aristocracy, and because he can give vent to his frustrations in this manner? And does not Gustchen express, in her illicit love affair, a contempt for her strict upbringing in a superficial society? Her words and pantomime suggest, in addition, that she has nymphomaniac tendencies which she cannot control.[22]

After the Major and his wife have learned of the daughter's seduction, Läuffer—now reduced to the spineless shadow of a man—is forced to flee and finds refuge in the home of an eccentric village schoolmaster named Wenzeslaus. Initially, the latter impresses us as being a healthy counterpart of Läuffer, who has adjusted to life and can rehabilitate his refugee-guest. Wenzeslaus—named Martin[23] in the original version—seemingly leads a contented, temperate life like Martin in Goethe's *Götz*, and like the latter figure, he sees the aristocracy from its brighter side. Indulging in the little pleasures of a pipe and a bottle of wine and some knockwurst, he appears happy eking out his meager existence in the manner of Jean Paul's Wuz two decades later. A colorful, complex personality, who comes to life in his authentic surroundings, he illustrates the theories of character portrayal in the *Anmerkungen*. With his loquaciousness and scurrilous behavior he anticipates the schoolmaster in Grabbe's *Scherz, Satire, Ironie und tiefere Bedeutung*. But underneath this colorful caricature who evokes laughter modern critics see in Wenzeslaus something of a frustrated, subhuman,[24] mentally diseased individual.[25] When he emotes ecstatically on hearing that the tutor has castrated himself, and when he tells Läuffer to sing in his helpless condition—"Ich bin der Nichtigkeit entbunden, nun Flügel, Flügel, Flügel her!"[26] ("I have been set free from nullity; now give me wings, wings, wings.")—we sense that we are dealing with a mental case. Lenz's characters betray themselves with every word and gesture, and Wenzeslaus's dialogue gives indication of being that of a befuddled mind. He repeats himself, and his speech is so filled with redundancies that it becomes tangled up and incoherent. Like Büchner's Woyzeck in the following century, his grotesque and dissonant dialogues suggest a most eccentric individual.[27]

Absurd as Läuffer's act of emasculation itself appears, we cannot imagine a more likely place for this bizarre act to occur than in the home of the schoolmaster. Läuffer, believing that Gustchen has committed suicide after giving birth to their illegitimate child, says that he has committed his outrageous act out of desperation and remorse. Schneider interprets the deed as drastic comedy, in which Lenz wants to express in a grotesque, satirical manner the Storm and Stress revolt against churchly asceticism.[28] But Max Spalter, more correctly, see Läuffer's behavior as logical, in terms of the psychopathology of character, as Lenz has developed it. According to Spalter, Läuffer has always chosen to be passive in order to avert any clash in the world of powerful social determinants. Confronted, for the first time, by a powerful, instinctual sexual urge which he obviously cannot control, he has taken drastic measures to prevent crises in the future and to maintain his passive nature.[29] In depicting man as a victim of his sexual drive, Lenz anticipates a common theme of twentieth-century drama, especially that of Wedekind. A sequel to the castration episode, the mutually contemplated marriage of Läuffer and the village maiden, Lise, which seems to lack in taste, must be interpreted ironically. In Läuffer's blighting social environment, where he is reduced to an automaton, a harmonious life, symbolized by love and marriage, is a very bad joke at best.

In closely following the fortunes of Läuffer we have violated the sequence and spirit of the drama as Lenz intended it. In reality, the Läuffer episodes are interspersed in a kaleidoscope of short scenes which shift abruptly from the aristocratic milieu of the Berg's, to the bohemian environment of student life, and to a shabby hut in the forest, as well as to the schoolmaster's abode. By violating the Aristotelian unities with utter abandon, Lenz has written a play which is highly distracting and, at times, borders on the chaotic. But this open structure does enable the author, in the manner of the Naturalists, to show slices of real life, in which the character's actions reflect a particular milieu. By putting his characters in authentic situations, Lenz has them act and react in such a way as to reveal the social and instinctual forces which drive them on. Above all we are made aware of a character's social status and the tremendous influence which the rigid class structure exerts on him.

Equally important as the content of these scenes is their arrangement. Although they are not always related to a main plot, these scenes juxtapose images of a particular stratum of society which repeat the same basic picture. Anticipating Brecht and the modern epic theater, Lenz employs a method of episodic reinforcement to nail down the point he is trying to make; namely, that man is a victim of a power struggle between the haves and the have-nots, and that finding a solution to this predicament is most difficult. On the one hand, there are the parasitic, callous, and stupid aristocrats who treat their inferiors with contempt; on the other, the servile, cowardly middle class, who can best adjust to their deplorable condition by remaining passive. Lenz's characters belong to one or the other of the two groups.

Läuffer's father, for instance, like his son, has no choice but to face the facts and get along with the aristocracy as best he can. He becomes the cringing, servile parson, who is ready to accept any humiliation to gain preferment. At the university, the students representing the middle class appear in a good light. They are a gay and carefree lot and evince a fierce loyalty to each other. But Pätus, like Läuffer, lacks independent means and is the butt of the jokes of the landladies, who prefer the rich and aristocratic Fritz von Berg. A victim of his instinctual urge, Pätus falls in love with every beautiful girl. Reduced to penury, thwarted in love, molded by society into a marionette, his grotesque condition is effectively depicted in the form of a caricature. Wearing a fur coat in the midsummer heat, chased through the streets by yelping dogs, with flushed face and hair flying,[30] he furnishes an excellent example of the characteristic, caricatured personality which Lenz advocates. That Pätus, primarily through Fritz von Berg's intercession, marries Jungfer Rehaar at the end does not change the image of him we have formed. Again the ending is an ironic twist, a manifest derision of the Philistine mentality. That the character of Pätus in many ways represents Läuffer and even Lenz himself and reinforces their attitude toward life is quite evident. Subplots built around minor personages like Pätus also have the effect of alienation, that is, Lenz's tendency to casually drop one thread of action and pick up another keeps us from getting close enough to a character to elicit our identification and sympathy. Another method Lenz uses to achieve alienation is to delineate a character such as Pätus in a humorous manner.

Lenz's habit—especially in the student scenes—of expressing character through names is worthy of note in passing. Here, too, the traits are conditioned by the stresses of a highly structured society. Thus the gay, frivolous tutor is called "Läuffer" and the fickle, irresponsible, aristocratic dandy's name is "Seiffenblase." The coquette who tries to exploit young Pätus is named "Hamster," and her friend betrays her servile position by answering to the name of "Knicks."

Just as students of the burgher class demonstrate anew in their behavior the foibles of the middle class noted in earlier scenes, so do the young aristocratic students, in their actions, provide reinforcement for the image of the upper class as it gradually comes into focus. Von Seiffenblase, a product of the decadent Rococo society, as represented earlier by the Major, his wife, and Count Wermuth, offers an additional example of privileged vice seeking to besmirch unprivileged virtue by attempting to seduce the burgher maiden, Miss Rehaar.

On the other hand, Fritz von Berg, a true son of his father, the Councillor, is a forthright, honest young man, who respects a person as a human being. Like his father, he is an idealist who believes that one can break the deterministic chain of events and bring about a rapprochement between the classes. His misfortune of being imprisoned for a short time stems from his being overly generous to his impoverished student friend and from failing to look at life realistically. Fritz von Berg shows Pietistic leanings, forgiving Gustchen and marrying her. To make amends for neglecting her while at the university, he will adopt her illegitimate child as his own and forget the past. Likewise, Gustchen, in her actions, illustrates the three stages of Pietism leading to deliverance—the fall, atonement, and salvation—approximately as they appear in two widely known novels of the time: Gellert's *Schwedische Gräfin* and Sophie La Roche's *Geschichte des Fräuleins von Sternheim*. Like Gustchen, Lise, the peasant girl in Wenzeslaus' village, injects a note of optimism. She is the simple, naïve, unspoiled child of nature, as Rousseau would have treasured her, who has compassion for the mentally and physically ailing Läuffer.

But projected against the grotesque background of the drama, these meliorating elements seem out of place; at best they reflect the inherent dualism in Lenz's approach to life. The idealistic cynic points, on the one hand, to a world in desperate need of reform and on the other to a society totally determined by conditions against which man is powerless to act. The Shakespearean episodic structure is ideally suited, through repetition and reinforcement, to graphically depict the milieu which forces man to keep spinning around on his own treadmill. In this atmosphere, man is confused and frustrated at the outset of the drama, is unable to learn from experience, and winds up quite ingloriously. The noble hero who suddenly becomes aware of untapped spiritual resources, as we encounter him in Schiller, would be totally out of place in Lenz's dramas. Characters like Läuffer and Wenzeslaus make no pretense to greatness. They are quite ordinary, prosaic individuals and illustrate, as do Büchner's characters in a later time, that art can work with the lowest materials.

In the last scene of the play, as at the beginning, Councillor Berg, as commentator and objective bystander, tries to convince us that he is still primarily concerned with the dangers of private education and their remedy. The reformer Lenz is still at work; but somehow the cynic lurking in the background is more convincing. He sees something irrevocably wrong with contemporary society and perhaps with the human condition itself.

III   Die Soldaten

In *Die Soldaten,* which appeared in 1776 and is undoubtedly Lenz's finest artistic creation, the theme of social reform again comes to the fore. In a programmatic dialogue between the Countess La Roche and Colonel von Spannheim in the final scene of the play, we learn ostensibly why the play was written in the first place: it was to point out a serious social problem and propose a solution for it. The enforced celibacy of the army officers has caused a flagrant social evil; namely, the burghers' virtuous daughters have been victimized by the frustrated soldiery. Agreeing to the seriousness of the state of affairs and the need for reform, the two principals mull over the causes and remedies, until the Colonel makes a proposal: the king should be prevailed upon to set up a school to train a corps of sexually compliant women—women who shall accompany the army and shall be held in high esteem for the sacrifice that they make for the general welfare of humanity. Actually this proposal, made at the end of the drama, represented the core of a document, "Uber die Soldaten Ehen," which Lenz presented to the Duke of Weimar and used as his excuse to visit this contemporary mecca of culture. Shocking as this reform plan is, it still makes more sense in pamphlet form than as a part of a drama; after reading a few scenes we realize that von Spannheim's proposal does not really relate to the drama proper or offer an appropriate solution. The social reformer Lenz uses his harebrained scheme ironically. He has, in reality, no meliorist convictions concerning social progress and equates the dismal social scene with his own inability to find harmony.

Observing the Storm and Stress tenets that true art is an imitation of nature, and as such is a genuine, national expression, Lenz connects the plot of *Die Soldaten* with his cultural environment and even with his own personal experiences. Although the scene of the play is laid in three towns of Flanders, it is in reality Strassburg and the Alsatian environs. In fact the disguise did not succeed completely, for at one place the word "Rheinluft" slips into the dialogue,[31] obviously from an earlier version of the play. The cast of characters, which is made up of the officers of the regiment and the family of Marie Wesener, clearly represents Lenz's social environment in Strassburg. Having lived with the Kleist brothers in the garrison towns of Strassburg and Landau, he had a firsthand knowledge of army life, and he was equally at home in the middle-class environment of the heroine. Indeed, the characters and the plot were so close to Lenz's own experiences that he withheld publication for a time, then decided to ascribe the drama to a "Steenkerk aus Amsterdam,"[32] only to have it appear in the last instant anonymously.

Although *Die Soldaten* follows the tradition of Diderot and Mercier by vividly depicting bourgeois life and problems with a view to initiate social reform, it is not this aspect of Lenz's work which has caught the attention of dramatists of succeeding generations. Rather it is the form which has made Lenz a pathfinder; it is his skillful use of the episodic structure, his ingenious blending of language, pantomime, caricature, and scenery to reveal the psyche of modern man, which has afforded him an ever greater prominence.

The drama centers about a middle-class girl, Marie Wesener. She is the younger daughter of a jeweler, who for mercantile reasons approves the contemplated marriage of his favorite child to a draper named Stolzius. Meanwhile the aristocratic officer, Desportes, courts her and wins her affection, because of the improved social position that the new relationship would seem to offer. Initially opposed to a union of members of different classes, the jeweler begins to look with favor on his daughter's conquest and the prospects of having a son-in-law from the aristocracy.

When all obstacles seem to have been removed for Marie, Desportes suddenly deserts her. In her efforts to find him and regain his affection, she befriends his aristocratic accomplice, Mary, only to sink lower in moral degradation. Stolzius, justifiably incensed by the turn of events, has resolved to take revenge, which culminates when he feeds poison to Desportes. Meanwhile Marie has plummeted deeper and deeper into mental depression and moral perversion, until at the end of the play her father finds her, a prostitute, begging for bread in the streets of a distant town. After this tearful, superemotional family reunion, a group of people carries both away. In the final scene, this unfortunate sequence of events is discussed by the Countess La Roche and Colonel von Spannheim, whose conversation culminates in the aforementioned preposterous proposal of the Colonel.

The plot consists of five acts and thirty-five scenes in which there are no less than thirty-four changes of the setting. The accelerated manner in which the author strings his scenes together, well illustrated in the fourth act, anticipates the technique used in Expressionism. Passing before our eyes in breathless haste these episodes, some only six words long, beginning with act four, scene four, communicate a sense of urgency on the part of all concerned, relative to Marie's sudden disappearance and the search for her. In succession we observe Desportes in the Armentières prison, fearful that Marie will find him and expose him to his family and colleagues; Marie's father at home, completely distraught upon learning that his daughter has run away; Stolzius in an identical frame of mind upon hearing the news and resolving to join the search; Marie's father and sister, reviewing the multiple but vain efforts to gain information, and fearing the worst; and finally, Desportes' rifleman, possessing a letter containing the best clue to her whereabouts, but ironically keeping this knowledge to himself for his own lustful purposes. And all five scenes occupy only one and one-half pages of text! It is the method of portrayal which is of cardinal importance and even supersedes the content. The sense of urgency and need for haste is not discussed or reported, it is conveyed by the rapid succession of scenes.

Lenz's utter disregard for unity of place, as illustrated by his abrupt shifts from one locale to another, is in conformity with the Storm and Stress proclivity to flaunt Aristotle and follow Shakespeare. The multiplicity of scenes has an intrinsic function as well. By shifting locales, Lenz is able to give us a rich social picture with a variety of social types interacting upon each other in an atmosphere where these relationships are genuine. Besides seeing Wesener at home and the officers in the surroundings of the familiar coffee house, we encounter father Wesener fumbling about in a strange town, a proud officer in jail, and catch glimpses of a Jew in his pawnshop and the Countess in the security of her ancestral home. The social environment enjoys great prominence in Lenz's dramas because his characters are, to such a great measure, molded by powerful social and economic determinants. Marie, the focal character in *Die Soldaten*, illustrates all too well the plight of a young woman caught in the web of forces from which she is not able to extricate herself.

Originally, Marie is a vivacious, personable young girl—"das beste liebenswürdigste Geschöpf,"[33] Countess La Roche calls her —who responds readily to the world she knows. In the first scene, believing that her fortune lies in the mercantile world in which she was born, she writes a "thank you" letter to the mother of her suitor, the draper Stolzius. Since she looks upon Stolzius with favor and he represents the same social stratum as her father, she uses the business-letter style of her father. The affected language, the omission of personal pronouns, and the use of stilted infinitives and Gallicisms reveal not only the language of the merchant per se, but also the inbred servility and the limited horizon of the class:

Meine liebe Matamm! Wir sein gottlob glücklich in Lille arriviert ... Wir wissen nicht, womit die Gütigkeit nur verdient haben, womit uns überschüttet, wünschte nur imstand zu sein ... Ihro alle die Politessen und Höflichkeit wieder zu erstatten. Weil aber es noch nicht in unseren Kräften steht, als bitten um fernere Kontinuation.[34]

My dear Madam: We arrived happily in Lille ... We are at a loss to know how we have deserved the kindnesses with which we were overwhelmed, would only wish to be in a position ... to repay you for all your politenesses and courtesies. But since it is not yet in our power, beg of you a delay in reciprocating.

Marie abruptly sheds the confines of her routine bourgeois existence when the officer, Baron Desportes, shows an interest in her and begins to court her. So avidly does she seek the status and power which the aristocracy can give her that she arranges a rendezvous with Desportes behind her father's back and rationalizes her actions by convincing herself that Desportes has only good intentions. Even father Wesener, a proud, irascible bourgeois personage reminiscent of Odoardo Galotti, forgets his initial distrust of the officer-suitor and is captivated by the prospect of having his daughter become a "lady." Marie, sensitive and intuitive as she is, realizes all too well that she is playing with fire, that she is up against powerful social forces, and that her origin is too low for her to become a due member of Desportes's circles. In her final speech at the end of the first act, her language and gestures reflect the tensions of a maiden who is cognizant of certain bitter social realities but who has not yet learned how to cope with them.

Marie's fears are not shared by Desportes. Formed from the same mold as the aristocrats in *Der Hofmeister,* he exemplifies the social parasite, the callous blueblood who is out to exploit the bourgeois maiden for his own gratification. Desportes's speech, like that of all characters in *Die Soldaten,* is most significant socially and expresses psychological nuances peculiar to him and his stratum. The excerpt below, taken from his dialogue with Marie, has an artificial ring about it. Containing the stilted, polite phraseology and sprinkling of Gallicisms common to Rococo culture, his words sound forced and insincere; but by cleverly feigning hurt pride and outrage, his argument seems credible to the gullible Marie:

Ich falsch? Können Sie das von mir glauben, göttliche Mademoiselle? Ist das falsch, wenn ich mich vom Regiment wegstehle, da ich mein Semestre doch verkauft habe und jetzt riskiere, dass, wenn man erfährt, dass ich nicht bei meinen Eltern bin, wie ich vorgab, man mich in Prison wirft, wenn ich wiederkomme, ist das falsch, nur um das Glück zu haben, Sie zu sehen, Vollkommenste?[235]

Me incincere? Can you believe that of me, my divine Mademoiselle? Is it being insincere, when I steal away from my regiment, now that I have sold half a year of service time, and run the risk of being thrown in prison, if someone discovers that I am not at my parents, as I alleged to be? Is it insincere when I come again, only to have the good luck of seeing you, my perfect one?

Marie's gullibility and inexperience show again when she is flattered by a poem Desportes has sent her, not realizing its highly sensual implications. The poem begins: "Du höchster Gegenstand von meinen reinen Trieben"[36] ("You, highest object of my pure [sex] drives"). Seen from Desportes's viewpoint this verse is laughable, but it forebodes tragic consequences for Marie.

Marie walks on a tightrope between middle-class tradition and morality on the one hand and aristocratic status and frivolity on the other. In the third scene of the second act she has not yet decided whether to cast her lot with the draper or with the aristocratic officer and has lost her identity in her predicament. Lenz brilliantly conveys her vacillating nature through her abruptly changing gestures and speech patterns. At the very outset, she is her true self, sitting in an easy chair and weeping, worrying about which course to follow. As Desportes enters unexpectedly, she hastily tries to hide a letter from Stolzius and in her perplexed state can only utter "Ach." In her second speech, she has already adopted a protective mask, and on mentioning the receipt and tone of Stolzius's letter, she assumes the defiant, remonstrating attitude of a typical small-town girl: "Sehen Sie nur, was mir der Mensch, der Stolzius schreibt, recht als ob er ein Recht hätte, mich auszuschelten" ("Just see what this fellow Stolzius writes, as if he had a right to scold me").

When Desportes hints at proposing marriage she becomes at once the virtuous maiden brought up in strict observance of middle-class traditions, who knows that it is folly to pursue idle dreams:

Nein, Herr Baron, davon wird nichts, das sind nur leere Hoffnungen, mit denen Sie mich hintergehen. Ihre Familie wird das nimmermehr zugeben.

No, Baron, nothing will come of that; those are only idle hopes with which you want to deceive me. Your family will never agree to that.

Marie assumes yet another mask after she indulges in some tomboyish horseplay with Desportes over the possession of a letter. Freed now from all inhibitions and filled with devilment, she addresses her father, who has just entered, in the coarse, ebullient, masculine language of the Storm and Stress genius:

Papa, denkt doch, was der grobe Flegel, der Stolzius, mir für einen Brief schreibt, er nennt mich Ungetreue! Denk doch, als ob ich die Säue mit ihm gehütet hätte; aber ich will ihm antworten darauf, dass er sich nicht vermuten soll, der Grobian.

Papa, just think what this clumsy boor of a Stolzius writes me in his letter! He calls me unfaithful! Just think, as though I had tended pigs together with him; but I'll answer him so that he won't be so presumptuous, the rude boy.

In this last speech Marie has unconsciously identified with Desportes in her use of language, and this identification continues in her dialogue with Jungfer Zipfersaat; in her high spirits she already imagines herself to be a baroness and expresses herself in the appropriate courtly language with its liberal use of French terms and Rococo niceties:

Jungfer Zipfersaat, hier habe ich die Ehre, dir einen Baron zu präsentieren, der sterblich verliebt in dich ist. Hier, Herr Baron, ist die Jungfer, von der wir soviel gesprochen haben, und in die Sie sich neulich in der Komödie so sterblich verschameriert haben.[37]

Miss Zipfersaat, I have the honor to present to you a Baron who is madly in love with you. Here, Baron, is the young lady of whom we have spoken so much, and with whom you were so infatuated recently at the comedy.

At the end of this scene, the dialogue dissolves into a blend of language, sound, gesture, pantomime, and rhythm, anticipating the non-verbal theater of Grabbe and Büchner. The frivolous laughter and antics of the two young lovers contrast grotesquely with the croaking voice of the tottering grandmother, and the discordant atmosphere seeems to portend an eerie gloom. Language and gesture anticipate as well the mood of the song which the old lady sings while knitting. Her lyrics, which tell of a young bride and her transitory blissful state, are a ballad of despair and give us a good idea of what is to come later in the drama. Life's ruthless determinism appears metaphorically in the first two lines of the song, where a young maiden is compared to dice on the table; it appears again in a stage direction between the first two stanzas, as the old grandmother is mechanically counting her stitches while knitting. In the next century, Grabbe and Büchner were to follow Lenz's practice of inserting into the midst of seemingly trivial dialogue short melodic verses with frightening and sinister overtones.

The eerie atmosphere surrounding Marie and the officer Desportes makes us surmise that no good can come of their relationship, that the depraved and unscrupulous Desportes has merely sought out the naïve middle-class girl to satisfy his sexual appetite. A flurry of scenes of army life only vaguely related to the plot nevertheless are important because they throw light on the eccentric social behavior of Desportes and his fellow officers. Not allowed to marry, living in a sexless limbo, and thoroughly bored with their unnatural existence, they indulge in a variety of pastimes, usually at the expense of the lower social stratum. We must not forget that the soldiers in this drama are really officers, who, in turn, stem from the aristocratic caste. As such they have the same callous disrespect for the middle class as does the nobility in *Der Hofmeister.*

In one scene, where the officers in their boredom get into a trivial conversation about the moral value of the theater,[38] their conduct is harmless enough; but in another episode, where the officers lure one of their colleagues, the sexually starved Rammler, into the home of a Jew, on the pretext of having arranged a liaison for him with a young Jewess, it is the Jew, Aaron, who is victimized, treated rudely, and almost scared out of his wits.[39] It is interesting to note that Aaron speaks in a Jewish dialect, testifying to Lenz's preoccupation with dialectal peculiarities and to his intense desire to create scenes true to life.

The speech of the officers has its own idiosyncrasies as well. We have already noted Desportes's Rococo style, which he uses when he wants to impress the middle class. But when the officers talk among themselves they prefer the exaggerated and bombastic language of the "Stümer und Dränger." This manner of speaking reflects not only the fashion of the times but also the temperament of the officers. Bored and frustrated, they frequently give vent to their emotions by using expressions having to do with maiming and destroying human life. Cases in point are Rammler's utterances: "Und ich brech' dir Arm und Bein entzwei und werf' sie zum Fenster hinaus"[40] ("And I'll break your arms and legs in pieces and throw them out the window") and "Ich will euch in Kreuzmillionen Stücke zerhauen"[41] ("I'll chop you up into millions of pieces"). In a similar vein, Haudy says: "Ich werd' dir das Genick umdrehen"[42] ("I'll break your neck"). The aristocratic officers are not averse to using coarse epithets to describe persons. Expressions like "Soldatenhure"[43] ("army whore") and "[Ihre] verfluchten Arschgesichter"[44] ("you damned ass faces") are typical. The simile used by Haudy, "Ja du steckst voll Finten wie ein alter Pelz voll Läuse"[45] ("You are full of tricks like an old fur full of lice") illustrates a colorful though hyperbolic and grotesque mode of expression. Dialectal and colloquial terms abound in the language of "genius," and in dialogues a preponderance of verbs attests to the unbridled energy emitted by the "Kraftkerls." Although Goethe in Götz and Klinger in his dramas treat the powerful Storm and Stress language sympathetically, it is obvious that Lenz satirizes it as well as the officers who speak it. The style which reflects Lenz's true nature is vastly different and is, as we shall see, best revealed in the distraught speech of Marie and Stolzius.

The officers' language is primarily that of a particular social structure, but in a few instances it also has intellectual implications. Pastor Eisenhardt and Colonel Spannheim personify eighteenth-century German Rationalism in their lucid and logical discussions. In the true spirit of the Age of Enlightenment, they stress the moralizing influence of the theater and evaluate a drama as being "useful" or "harmful."[46] In order to exhibit as many types as possible in the "Raritätenkabinett" of his century, Lenz also introduces an extreme Rationalist in the person of Pirzel. While Eisenhardt and von Spannheim are depicted as objectively and sympathetically as is possible for a man of genius, Pirzel does not fare so well. His speech, like that of every Lenz character, betrays his personality—a pompous Philistine of low intelligence. Pursuing Rationalistic thinking to its extreme, he can only utter banalities and inanities to fill an intellectual void. A repetitive expression of his: "Das [Denken] geht so mechanisch"[47] ("It [thinking] is all so mechanical") exemplifies his mentality.

Stolzius, who suffers so unjustly at the hands of the officers, is, in contrast to Pirzel, close to Lenz's heart. In fact, Werner Wien, who wrote a critical study on Lenz, feels that in Stolzius the author has drawn a portrait of himself in his Strassburg days;[48] taken from this same environment Cleophe Fibich becomes Marie, and the Kleist brothers her seducers transformed into the

literary personages of Desportes and Mary.[49] Stolzius, who had
lived happily and peaceably in his bourgeois environment, suddenly loses his identity when an unimplicated gossiper in the
coffee house hints strongly that Marie has betrayed him. Lamed
in spirit and feeling completely alienated from the world, he at
first becomes a recluse who is unable to function anymore. He
descends to the level of a soldier-servant to carry out the only
mission he feels is left for him—revenge.

In his emotional crises, as for example when he stands before
the apothecary getting up enough nerve to buy poison to kill
Desportes, his speech is an effective blend of gesture, mimetic
language, poignant mood, and authentic idiom:

[*Stolzius geht vor einer Apotheke herum.*] Was zitterest du?—Meine
Zunge ist so schwach, dass ich fürchte, ich werde kein einziges Wort
hervorbringen können. Er wird mir's ansehen—und müssen denn die
zittern, die Unrecht leiden, und die allein fröhlich sein, die Unrecht
tun?—Wer weiss, zwischen welchem Zaun sie jetzt verhungert. Herein,
Stolzius. Wenn's nicht für ihn ist, so ist's doch für dich. Und das ist
ja alles, was du wünschest—[50]

(*Stolzius walks back and forth in front of an apothecary.*) Why do
you tremble?—My tongue is so weak that I fear I will not be able to
utter a single word. He'll notice it—and must those tremble who suffer
injustice, and only those be happy who commit injustices?—Who
knows along what fence she is starving to death now. Come in, Stolzius. If it is not for him, it's for you. And that is all that you wish for.

The above passage, typical of the distraught speech of Stolzius
and Marie,[51] is significant because it reveals Lenz's true style,
which he pioneered and which became a prototype for Büchner,
Grabbe, and more recent German dramatists. It is incisive, terse,
and reserved; it intimates pent-up emotion without expressing it,
and depends heavily on gesture for its full effect. Büchner not
only imitates Lenz's style, but the literal content of his drama as
well. Büchner's Wozzek and Marie, like Stolzius and Marie
Wesener, are buffeted about by similar deterministic conditions,
until the male protagonist commits murder out of desperation.
Stolzius, painfully aware that an aristocratic officer has made his
fiancée, Marie, his pawn, and cognizant that justice is impossible
in this severely class-structured society, must take his own life as
well as Desportes's.

As in *Der Hofmeister*, the enlightened aristocracy, which is

atypical and outnumbered (and represented in *Die Soldaten* by
Countess La Roche), makes a determined but ironically inade-
quate effort to avert tragedy. The Countess reacts to rumors that
the commoner Marie has been led astray by young aristocrats,
including her son, by inviting Marie to come to live with her,
with the hope of restoring her respectability. Practicing the
tenets of her Pietistic religion, the Countess believes that a person can be morally changed for the better through education and
religious atonement. Besides her deeds her speech reflects her
Pietistic leanings. In her conversation, expressions dealing with
heart, emotion, excessive feeling, and sentimentality abound:
"empfindliches Herz" ("sensitive heart") . . ."Herzensangelegen-
heiten"[52] ("affairs of the heart") . . ."Imagination"("imagination")
. . ."fühlen" ("to sense") . . ."Phantasie" ("fantasy").[53] Typical,
too, are these expressions reflecting a tender, delicate, sympathetic, and intensely personal tone: "sachte"[54] ("gentle") . . .
"zärtliche Freundin" ("tender friend") . . ."Mitleid"[55] ("sympathy"). . ."nehmen Sie meinen heissesten Dank in dieser Träne"[56]
("accept my warmest thanks in this tear").

In chiding her son for not treating a servant with more respect,[57] she is anticipating a sympathetic concern for the lowest
social stratum as evinced in Büchner and Brecht. Progressive in
this respect, she shows herself, nevertheless, to be ultraconserva-
tive in wanting to maintain strict class distinctions. She reproaches Marie for entertaining the idea of marriage with an
officer who comes from a higher class. Yet her dialogue takes on
a very human tone when she sympathizes with Marie for having
human inclinations: "I don't know whether I can in good conscience deprive the girl of her romance. What charm does life
hold if we don't rely on our fantasy? Eating, drinking, hopeless
preoccupations without self-created gratification are only a slow
death."[58] Thus, in an unguarded moment, the Countess recognizes the instinctual sexual urge which so strongly affects man's
conduct. This scene, as well as the previous meeting between the
Countess and Marie at the close of Act III, has an open ending,
which is so typical for Lenz, Büchner, Wedekind, the Expressionists, and their followers. That is, the chief character—in this
case Marie—has several alternatives to follow. As a sensitive and
volatile young girl who acts on impulse and is the prey of her
emotions, which she cannot discipline, she will naturally follow

the road leading to her lover; while as the well-bred burgher maiden who was newly instructed in the ways of Pietistic repentance and forgiveness she will atone for her sins. Actually, the problematic and Lenzian character she is, she tries both methods.

Like Gustchen in *Der Hofmeister*, Marie follows a three-step Pietistic formula leading to deliverance. Flirting with the aristocratic officers and succumbing to their wiles naturally represents the fall; falling on her knees before the Countess, with hands folded,[59] she assumes the classic stance to begin atonement; trudging along the road to Armentières as a tired, destitute, and starving beggar, she has sufficiently expiated her sins to gain pardon. Somehow this religious, meliorist interpretation seems incongruous with the general tone of the drama. Though Lenz had strong Pietistic leanings, especially in his youth, they were not sufficient to sustain him personally amid the demonic forces he encountered.

An impulsive Marie, whose actions are irrevocably determined by external social conditions, would seem to represent Lenz's views more accurately. By means of an episodic structure, in which a multiplicity of scenes serve to depict Marie's milieu concretely and fully, she is presented as a person molded by fate who is unable to act differently than she does. Catered to by the young aristocrats, she is so obsessed by the idea of rising socially and gaining status, that she loses her sense of values. Naïve enough to believe that she is entitled to enjoy life as much as the officers, she is oblivious to social realities. Marie does not want to accept Lenz's premise in *Der Hofmeister* and *Die Soldaten* that a chasm separates the callous, parasitic haves from the gullible, servile, victimized have-nots, and that not much can be done to bridge the gap. From this standpoint, Marie's efforts have to be regarded as ironic. The scene where she and her father embrace feverishly in mutual delirium, an ending suggesting Pietistic deliverance, does not ring true. Rather, Marie would seem to be closer to the mark, as the tragic victim of circumstance, whose spirit is broken, whose hopes are shattered, who despairs of life in an atmosphere of gloomy twilight. Countess La Roche and Colonel von Spannheim, appearing as commentators in the last scene, in an effort to prevent subsequent tragedies offer a simple, idealistic solution. The cynic Lenz knows it to be hopelessly inappropriate.

IV   Der neue Menoza

Between *Der Hofmeister* and *Die Soldaten* Lenz wrote another social satire, *Der neue Menoza*. It differs from the previously discussed dramas primarily because it is not based directly on personal experiences and because it is written in a lighter vein, intended to be pure comedy. It may be that Lenz subconsciously felt the need for a pleasant, diversionary interlude, where he could still attack social and cultural evils without becoming maniacally involved. As the innovator Lenz was in his efforts to pioneer new paths in the field of German comedy, he went beyond the traditional Saxon comedy for his inspiration. In the two final scenes of *Der neue Menoza*, the author himself is speaking in the person of the mayor of Naumburg, when the latter wishes to see a puppet play because of its fresh, rejuvenating effect. It is to the puppet theater that Lenz goes for new ideas, as well as to the coarse comedy of the folk theater; going even further back in the history of comic theater, Lenz draws thematic and structural ideas from the Commedia dell'arte and its spiritual forebears, the comedies of Plautus.

The direct literary source of Lenz's drama was a Danish novel written by Erich Pontoppidan in 1743, which received wide currency in Germany through a translation. Entitled *Menoza, ein asiatischer Prinz ,welcher die Welt umher gezogen, Christen zu suchen, aber des Gesuchten wenig gefunden,* the novel's Protestant-orthodox inclinations did not lend themselves to a Storm and Stress temperament. Lenz borrows from Pontoppidan only some external details. Moreover, he projects the motif of the exotic traveler into a Rousseau-oriented world for the purpose of putting contemporary civilization to the test.

Lenz's new Menoza was born in Europe, but at an early age was taken by a Jesuit mission to Asia; smiled on by fortune, he fared well in the kingdom until he was named successor to the throne. Just as rapidly his luck changed, until he was glad to escape the foreign land with his life. He arrives in Germany, not as a primitive, but as a sensitive, educated person, who is schooled in the ideas of Rousseau and in the use of objective reason. Invited to Naumberg by the stalwart citizen von Biederling, he expects to find in this typically European atmosphere, "truth, greatness, and kindness,"[60] to use Lenz's words from his own critical defense, but encounters just the opposite. Originally Menoza (henceforth called Prince Tandi) plans to remain the objective bystander, but after he falls in love with von Biederling's daughter, Wilhelmine, he loses this privileged position and becomes directly involved in the wildest intrigues and most depraved situations imaginable.

Count Camäleon and Donna Diana, a Spanish countess, are the evil forces and the catalysts who cause the greatest confusion. Although they are married, the principals of the play are never aware of it, which adds to their bewilderment. Donna Diana has had her father poisoned for material reasons, and the Count shows his moral perversion by courting Wilhelmine. Wilhelmine, however, intuitively loves Prince Tandi and accepts his proposal. No sooner are they married than a major surprise —by no means the last one—catches the characters and the audience completely unawares: von Zopf, an acquaintance of von Biederling, informs Prince Tandi and Wilhelmine that they are brother and sister. Tandi is actually the long-lost son of the Biederlings. Completely numbed by the idea that he is guilty of incest, Tandi leaves town to forget and do penance. Von Biederling and his friends, on the other hand, try to circumvent the law and its ethical implications to preserve their marriage. Meanwhile Donna Diana, bent on revenge, uses a masked ball to foil Count Camäleon. Disguised as Wilhelmine, she stabs him to death when he makes improper advances to her. In a shocked state of mind, Donna's nurse, Babet, reveals what turns out to be the second major secret: Donna was exchanged as an infant and is really von Biederling's daughter, and Wilhelmine is really Donna, the daughter of a Spanish Count. This turn of events removes all complications for Prince Tandi and his wife and allows for a happy ending. Such is the confused and turbulent action which makes up the plot. The last two scenes of *Der neue Menoza* record a rather diversionary dialogue between a university graduate, Zierau, and his father, concerning the three dramatic unities and the values of marionette plays.

Lenz himself referred to *Der neue Menoza* as a "rushed play"[61] although its haphazard and disorderly nature very likely reflects Lenz's temperament rather than fate of circumstance. Contemporary criticism, which followed the drama's publication in 1774, was almost unanimously critical of its chaotic nature and its chances for success on the stage.[62] Although there is no denying the presence of discordant elements in the drama, there would still appear to be a certain organic unity in the structure which has been well-nigh overlooked. Specifically, *Der neue Menoza* may be said to illustrate a gradual progression from a negative to a positive attitude, from rather passive social satire to an effective program of action. And as a corollary of this idea, the drama traces man's development from an artificial, fettered, and decadent state to his true, uninhibited, and genuine nature.

As the drama unfolds, Prince Tandi has spent only a short time as von Biederling's guest in Naumberg, when he wants to go back to Asia. What repels him is "indolence, lazy, feeble desire, babbling death instead of fire and life, idle talk instead of action."[63] Expressing his further disappointment at the European society and its decadent and superficial attitude toward life, he continues: "What you call sensitivity is disguised lust; what you call virtue is makeup with which you cover up brutality."[64] Lenz uses colorful characters as vehicles for satirizing specific social and cultural shortcomings. In the student Zierau, a descendant of the boastful Capitano of the Commedia dell'arte, he ridicules the spirit of Enlightenment and the veneration for Wieland. To Zierau, art, culture, and society have reached their zenith in his time. Wieland's *Goldener Spiegel*, Zierau says, is the crowning achievement of this age, singing the praises, as it does, of the perfect state in the form of enlightened absolutism.[65]

In the scholar Beza, bearing traits of the comical archetype, the Dottore, Lenz created not only a laughable but despicable character. The first time he appears[66] he is merely a killjoy, a narrow-minded Pietist who frowns on any merriment in this vale of tears. But in a later scene[67] he demonstrates that his stern Pietism is mere hypocrisy. When Prince Tandi discovers that his new wife is his sister and suffers remorse and consternation, Beza employs his scholarship in an insidious and morally repulsive manner to make an incestuous marriage appear legal and credible. As the servile burgher, who will forfeit his integrity to ingratiate himself to his superior, Beza reminds one of Läuffer's father in *Der Hofmeister*. We must point out, though, that in *Der neue Menoza* there is no tragic confrontation between the middle class and the aristocracy, as was the case in the previously discussed dramas. This time Lenz deals, with few exceptions, with the nobility and is as interested in cultural short-comings as in the foibles of a particular stratum of society.

With the exception of Prince Tandi, no one escapes the barbs of Lenz's satire. The representatives of contemporary German society—von Biederling, his wife, his daughter Wilhelmine, Count Camäleon, and Donna Diana—all have a common human failing: an egotistical desire to enjoy life, come what may, and imperviousness to higher moral considerations. Von Biederling is the blustering father, the comical Pantalone in burgher's clothes. Like Lessing's Tellheim he is a discharged officer, whose sense of humor, however, is treated in a completely humorous fashion. Although he follows some foolish whims and his horizon does not extend beyond Saxony, he is still treated more sympathetically than his cohorts. Von Biederling's wife is an old coquette in the vein of the Major's wife in *Der Hofmeister,* who succumbs to the calculated flattery of her daughter's suitor. The daughter, Wilhelmine, is a typical sentimental maiden of the eighteenth century. Lapsing into unconsciousness at every suitable opportunity, she is, in the words of her father, a fragile "paper creation."[68]

In Count Camäleon Lenz continues the practice of *Der Hofmeister* of expressing character through names. The Count is a fickle, vacillating person in the manner of Weislingen in Goethe's *Götz.* Incidentally, Donna Diana and the Count's servant, Gustav, likewise show remarkable affinity to the Goethean prototypes in the same drama, Adelheid and Franz. For the creation of the Count, Lenz owes a debt as well to the Saxon comedy of Christian Weise. Just as in the prototype, Lenz's Count leaves his wife and exhibits lustful desires for the daughter of his tenant. Lenz ostensibly wants to depict in Camäleon demoralized, decadent Europe in the Rococo age. Gestures and mimetic speech help in revealing his true nature.

Camäleon's wife and female counterpart, Donna Diana, continues the tradition of the "Machtweib" represented earlier by Lessing's Orsina and Goethe's Adelheid. Upon learning that the Count has deceived her and is in love with Wilhelmine, she becomes a raging fury, carried along by uninhibited passions and instinctual urges, unable to control her emotions:

Was? Wenn der Graf—red aus, wenn der Graf—wenn er sie liebt, wenn er sie heiratet—ich will ihn verwirren, verzweifeln, zerscheitern durch meine Gegenwart. Wie ein Gott will ich erscheinen, meine Blicke sollen Blitz sein, mein Odem Donner—lass uns unterwegens davon reden, es ist mir Wonne, wenn ich davon reden kann. Er soll in seinem Leben vor keinem Menschen, vor Gott dem Allmächtigen nicht so gezittert haben—die verächtliche Bestie![69]

What? If the count—finish it, if the count—if he loves her, if he marries her—I want to confuse him, drive him to despair, wreck him by my presence. Like a God I want to appear; my glances shall be as lightning, my breath thunder—let us talk about it on the way; it will be a joy to me if I can talk about it. In his whole life he shall never have trembled before man, before God the Almighty in such a manner—the despicable beast!

This exaggerated and bombastic speech is alien to Lenz's temperament and normal mode of expression, just as was the dialogue of the officers in *Die Soldaten*. In both cases, he intends to satirize the Storm and Stress style, which, though popular at the time, was personally repulsive to him. Donna Diana's caricatured personality has a satirical function as well, serving to expose intrigue, treachery, and ruthlessness, which Lenz felt were rampant in Rococo society.

Satirical depiction of character, which is stressed in the first half of the drama, quite understandably cannot have much to do with plot progression or with the propulsion of the main theme: the development of Prince Tandi from an impassive bystander to an actively involved individual. In fact, Prince Tandi is so repelled by the social milieu exemplified by the drama's principals that he is about to leave Europe. At this critical juncture, his sudden, impulsive desire to possess and marry Wilhelmine involves him involuntarily and emotionally with the new civilization. It is the emotional factor which assumes prime importance not only in determining Prince Tandi's subsequent development, but in initiating the drama's motivating forces, and—what is of cardinal importance—in providing the framework for the scenes themselves.

In a recent study, Hinck has analyzed the structure of *Der neue Menoza* and found an astonishing similarity in the construction of twelve main scenes.[70] Each of these espisodes has an emotional shock as its nucleus. At the outset of the scene, a sensitive, high-strung individual is enjoying, for the time being, an almost idyllic security. Just when his inner defenses are down and he least expects anything to happen, he receives the shock treatment. Caught unawares, he gravitates from one extreme emotional state to one that is diametrically opposite. This span between the two eccentric states of mind embraces the gamut of human feeling from its most ecstatic joys to its lowest existential depths. The shocks or explosion, usually in the form of news communicated by an outsider, sets off emotional repercussions which persist until the end of the scene. The repercussions take on a variety of forms such as fright, anger, emotive joy, physical paralysis, and impetuous gestures. The scene closes with an open ending which we have come to recognize as a trademark of Lenz. In an atmosphere of consternation and frustration, the character must face the world by making one of several possible decisions.

To illustrate the structure outlined above, the third scene of the third act, disclosing Tandi's and Wilhelmine's incestuous relationship, may serve as a cogent example. In the relaxed and intimate atmosphere of the sitting room, Prince Tandi and Wilhelmine engage in the gay and carefree banter of a young couple in love. Suddenly, Herr von Zopf, a friend of von Biederling, appears at the door and immediately imparts to them what he innocently considers to be welcome news: they are brother and sister. Wilhelmine, sensing that she will be forever parted from her lover, in succession falls down on the sofa, lapses into unconsciousness, kicks von Zopf in anger, threatens to kill him with his own dagger, and in her delirium asks von Zopf to turn the dagger on her. Gesture and pantomime blend effectively with language to communicate her emotional state. Prince Tandi is so stunned by the shocking news that he can only utter a laconic: "Lass mich [gehen]!" ("Let me go!").[71] Flight to a place where he can think must offer him temporary respite. Thus the scene ends in turmoil. The lovers would like to be united, but fear that this is impossible.

Such concentration of the stage action on mimetically charged shock situations is a structural trait of the Commedia dell'arte. As in the Commedia dell'arte, a specific situation can stand by itself; most likely, however, it will start a chain reaction of related situations. In any event, the shock situation provides the dramatic framework of the play; expressed in another way, the startling event forms the nucleus of a situation comedy and of a series of related situation comedies. The shock situation in *Der neue Menoza* is not made possible, as it is in the Italian masked comedy, through comical character reinforcement, nor through comically stubborn persistence in denying the true state of affairs, but through accidental provocation of passionate feelings.

It is this emotional element which, as stated above, becomes the decisive factor, linking the satirical, structural, and ethical components of the play into an organic whole. Through a series of traumatic experiences, in which Prince Tandi is shaken to the very depths and his emotions are set free, he gradually changes from a passive bystander to an individual possessing the laudable qualities of "fire, life and action."[72] Strange though it may seem, these are internal rather than external qualities. By liberating his emotional self, the Prince begins to feel that passive criticism of a decadent external world is fruitless; that man must, instead, throw off the shackles of a sterile civilization and of hypocrisy to arrive at the only true value—one's genuine inner self. This true inner core appears to be a composite of intense feeling, instinct, and conscience. Upon regaining these attributes of primitive man, the Rousseau-oriented Prince exults "Mein wiedergefundenes Leben" ("I have regained my life") and Wilhelmine, in like manner, "Meine wiedergefundene Seele" ("I have regained my soul").[73] The other major characters undergo a similar transformation when a series of startling events cause them to bare their souls and expose all manner of deception and intrigue.

The structural framework of the drama, as outlined above, demands an episodic arrangement of scenes and a liberal change of locale. It is only through an unrelenting series of traumatic happenings, in the form of brief episodes, that the characters are forced to loose their emotions and to shed all illusion. And a particular environment, which is unique to the episode at hand, serves to intensify the emotional shock. For instance, an enchanted moonlit garden is the place where the Prince discovers his beloved one resisting the advances of an ardent suitor. To cite another example, it is in a festive hall that the murderer stalks the Count.

It is with express purpose that Lenz disregards the unity of time as well. From the outset, we have no idea when Prince Tandi was entrusted by his parents to the care of Herr von Zopf, or when and why the Jesuit mission brought him to Asia. From

the beginning, dates in the past are blurred and no specific
time intervals are mentioned during the course of the action. In
this fairy-tale atmosphere, there must needs be a lack of causal-
ity. All is based on chance and caprice, as is fitting for Lenz's
marionette figures, who dance about in a deterministic world.

An unreal and fairy-tale-like atmosphere was conducive to the
Commedia dell'arte, because this type of play depended primarily on genuine comic traits of the actors to be effective. In the
case of *Der neue Menoza,* the characters are not always comic,
nor are they convincing as lifelike members of a particular society. Consequently, the play never enjoyed great success on the
stage. Fabricated from his imagination and not based on genuine
experiences of the author, *Der neue Menoza* nevertheless contains a few realistic touches. Unfortunately, their occurrence is
so spotty and inconsistent that they are incongruous with respect
to the drama as a whole. We are told that the action takes place
in Saxony, but we are never supplied with enough local color to
make the avowed location credible. Von Biederling appears, at
the beginning, as a colorful German burgher, but he deteriorates
later into a vague stereotype. At the masked ball, a fat fellow,
anxious to help a lady in distress, expresses himself impulsively
in dialect: "Ich will sie [die Tür] uffrennen"[74] ("I want to force
open the door"). Yet other characters from the same social class
and in similar situations always speak the formal language of
the stage.

There are other incongruities which detract from the play's
artistic unity. While the love affair between Prince Tandi and
Wilhelmine is, on the whole, portrayed lyrically and sentimen-
tally, a grotesque interlude breaks the mood intermittently. In
one episode, the Prince is pining for his beloved in a coffee
house surrounded by an assemblage of beggars, rabble, lamed,
blinded, and hunchbacked people.[75] Though Lenz was bent on
writing a light comedy, the torment of his personal contradictions seems to have forced its way into his art unconsciously.
Other elements which disturb esthetically are, paradoxically
enough, caused by the very vehicle which was supposed to give
the play unity—the mechanism of the shock situation. The shock
must induce in the characters emotional feelings sufficient
enough to bring on frenzied rage, fainting fits, or the like. In
these extreme states, unfortunately, the individual often turns

into a ridiculous caricature or marionette, and what should be an emotionally charged situation is often reduced to a laughable one.

Although Lenz's use of caricature and marionette figures was not always successful, it did signify a pioneer attempt to introduce elements of the Commedia dell'arte into German comedy. Thematically, the intrigues stemming from impersonations, the confusions caused by mistaken identity, and the allied motif of the return of the person presumed dead, owe a similar debt to the Italian stage. Long before Stranitzky, Raimund, and Nestroy, Lenz recognized in the Commedia dell'arte a wellspring to infuse new life into the German comedy. *Der neue Menoza* is rich in fantasy, and the novel structure of its situation comedy aroused the interest of Clemens Brentano,[76] although he had reservations about the over-all effect of the play. Perhaps it never caught the fancy of the theatergoers because Lenz lacked the temperament to make a comedy come alive. Viewing existence as basically incongruous, he felt more at home in the realm of tragicomedy. Here comic derision could exist side by side with existential anguish, and the humorous could blend with the grotesque.

Lenz never again achieved the degree of artistry he had realized in *Der Hofmeister* and *Die Soldaten*. *Die beiden Alten* (1776) treats, in an unabashedly sentimental manner, a theme used later in Schiller's *Räuber:* a dissolute son has his aged and wealthy father imprisoned in order to come by his wealth. Virtue is crassly identified with the middle class, and vice with the nobility. In the same year there appeared *Die Freunde machen den Philosophen,* a remarkably exaggerated self-portrait. Strephon, a young German in Algiers, loves a lady of higher rank whom he dare not possibly hope to marry. Filled with burning passions, he gets relief from his frustrated longings and desires through fantasies and dreams. The happy ending is reminiscent of that of Goethe's *Stella,* which had just been completed. Although the drama reflects Lenz's frustrating love affair with Henriette von Waldner, he fails to give real relevance to the situations in which he puts his characters.

Lenz's last finished drama, *Der Engländer* (1777), arose from the same hopeless love for Henriette, but this time the conflict is solved by suicide. Since the action is overshadowed by the rich inner life of the hero, the play assumes the character of a lyrical monologue. The hero, Robert Hot, possesses the abnormal emotions and incurable obsessions of Lenz himself, and it is not surprising that in the suicidal fantasies of this drama he exhausted his creative talents.

Although Lenz was a member of the Storm and Stress movement, he was, even among the eccentric young geniuses, in many respects a "loner." No one felt the compulsive need to pioneer in style and structure more than he did; and no one shared his existential anguish or his cynical despair. Since his literary works are a search for man's true nature amid the grotesque paradoxes of life, his writings have struck a particularly responsive chord with modern dramatists, who are seeking similar solutions.

CHAPTER 3

Heinrich Leopold Wagner:
A Life in the Shadow of Greatness

LIKE LENZ, his personal acquaintance from the Strassburg days, Wagner used the stage to voice social concern. Both dramatists laid great stress on depicting the milieu realistically and precisely because, to them, man's essentially tragic condition was caused by powerful social determinants inherent in his environment. They saw the task of the dramatist as being one of identifying these deterministic forces and of attempting to neutralize them in the climate of public opinion. While Lenz was able to give deeper insight into the tragic contradictions of life by assigning them personal and even cosmic significance, Wagner remains, in contrast, on a superficial level, never penetrating beyond the realm of contemporary and tendentious problems. Schneider actually calls Wagner the "Sudermann" of the Storm and Stress dramatists.[1] Like his nineteenth-century successor, Wagner wrote plays that are stageworthy, displaying, as they do, a keen sense for theatrical effect. He excelled, like Sudermann, in giving an impression of reality and in creating highly dramatic scenes from real life.

Wagner, the oldest of the "Goetheaner," was born in Strassburg in 1747. The son of a merchant of meager circumstances, he attended the local schools and university. Although the Goethe-Herder friendship of 1770 transformed this insular, provincial town into an important literary and cultural center, it is unlikely that Wagner enjoyed more than a casual relationship with Goethe and his circle at this time. By 1772, when Goethe had already left Strassburg, Wagner was just beginning to make his presence felt in the literary circle presided over by Salzmann, which had such a strong formative influence on the Storm and Stress movement.

At the university, Wagner, like Goethe, was enrolled in the faculty of law, although he, too, showed little enthusiasm for his major field of concentration. His first love was literature, and a collection of poems in the Anacreontic style marks his first attempt to write creatively. Unfortunately a Puritanically minded censor named Brackenhofer denied permission for publication of the lyrics because of their erotic and sensual tone. Since his family had become financially destitute, Wagner was forced to interrupt his studies in 1773 and accept a position as tutor in Saarbrücken, in the home of the President von Günderode. Most of Wagner's extant letters date from his two-year stay in Saarbrücken; they describe an affluent, congenial, and hospitable atmosphere. The literary attempts from this period still have an Anacreontic ring and include occasional poems to celebrate births, weddings, and deaths; mythological travesties; and popular ballads. Wagner's enthusiasm for Wieland furnishes ample proof that the revolutionary program of the Storm and Stress had as yet made little impression on him. The death of his benefactor forced Wagner to pull up roots once more.

In search of a livelihood, he went to Giessen, Darmstadt, and Frankfurt; and in his trek he crossed the paths of the young geniuses. It was in Frankfurt, where he was hired, for a time, as an assistant to a Professor Thompson, that he met Goethe once more and became more intimately acquainted with him. In *Dichtung und Wahrheit* Goethe calls Wagner

A good fellow, who was a member of our group, although he possessed no extraordinary talents. . . . I related to him, among other things, my intentions with *Faust,* especially the Gretchen episode. . . . He took it all in and used the central theme for his tragedy, *Die Kindsmörderin.*[2]

It was always Goethe's contention that Wagner was guilty of plagiarizing and that *Die Kindsmörderin* was an outright imitation of his Gretchen tragedy. Another work by Wagner, the farce, *Prometheus, Deukalion, und die Rezensenten* (1775) contributed to a cooling of relations between the two men. Although it was written in praise of the spirit of genius, it contained sufficient coarse indiscretions and tactless elements to prove embarrassing to the poet who had popularized the Prometheus symbol in the first place and with whom that literary symbol was automatically associated. A parody of Goethe's poem, *Der unverschämte Gast,* which appeared anonymously in the *Frankfurter Gelehrte Anzei-*

gen, but was believed to be a product of Wagner's pen, helped to bring about the final rupture.[3] Wagner seems to have been unwilling to subordinate himself to the leadership of the proud genius of the young Goethe, exhibiting, as he did, the same envy toward his superior as Lenz.

Although the sources for an accurate judgment are meager, the image Wagner projects in relation to his fellow men is not a pleasing one. Erich Schmidt finds him to have been equivocal and untrustworthy. He had a propensity for becoming involved in literary scandals and for writing malicious pamphlets. Because of his vanity, he considered himself an expert in a bewildering variety of literary and cultural activities, which prevented him from concentrating his talents and achieving true excellence in any one area. In the few letters that have been preserved, he suggests chameleon-like characteristics. When he writes to Boie he sounds overly affected; to Ring, a superior in law practice, he appears modest; to the actor Grossman he writes frivolously; and toward Maler Müller he adopts the exaggerated, bombastic tone of Storm and Stress.[4]

In the literary mecca of Frankfurt, Wagner met some of the leading men of his day: Boie, Klopstock, Mathias Claudius, and Wieland. He was a welcome guest in Klinger's home in Frankfurt, enjoying the friendship of the latter's mother and daughters as well. To the end of his life, Goethe's mother maintained cordial relations with him, even though her son did not. He became acquainted with Claudius in 1776 in the neighboring town of Darmstadt and maintained close relations with him. When, in the summer of 1776, he returned to Strassburg to complete his law studies and obtain his doctorate, he rejoined Salzmann's literary group. On July 18 this society, which at Lenz's instigation now was called "Deutsche Gesellschaft in Strassburg," discussed and gave its approval to Wagner's new play, *Die Kindsmörderin.* The enthusiasm for this tendentious drama was also shared by a fellow Storm and Stress exponent, Maler Müller, whom Wagner met in Mannheim on the way to Strassburg and whose friendship he treasured until his death. Wagner carried on a correspondence with another kindred spirit, the poet and musician Christian Schubart, who, as an older man, threw himself heart and soul into the movement.

Returning to Frankfurt after a fruitful summer, Wagner took his oath of office as a lawyer on September 21, 1776. Two weeks later he married a widow eighteen years his senior, whom he lost in death in May, 1778. Although he had acquired considerable popularity as an author with the publication of the farce *Prometheus*, the dramas *Die Reue nach der Tat* and *Die Kindsmörderin*, and the Mercier translation, *Neuer Versuch über die Schauspielkunst*, after 1776 Wagner appears to have been primarily interested in the stage itself. When the National Theater of Mannheim was being established, Goethe, Klinger, and Müller recommended him as a consultant to the authorities concerned.

Wagner acquired his greatest theatrical reputation as a member of the Seyler troupe of actors, the leading professional company in Germany. Serving as impromptu poet, producer, dramatist, translator, and legal counsel, he was completely engrossed in the performing arts. One of the memorable stage successes of the Seyler troupe was Wagner's version of Shakespeare's *Macbeth*, which was in essence the Wieland-Eschenburg translation updated to conform to the Storm and Stress style and temperament. Shakespeare's characters are completely uninhibited, speaking in a raucous voice and making the most of coarse expressions and mannerisms.[5] In 1777, obviously imitating Lessing in title and format, Wagner published the *Briefe, die Seylersche Schauspielergesellschaft betreffend*. The similarity is only skin deep, because Wagner's letters pursue no clearly defined goal and lack the unified esthetic theory inherent in Lessing's work. Wagner is content, for the most part, with giving long synopses of the plays, and praising the actors indiscriminately, without bothering to evaluate their individual performances. Enjoying the intimate friendship of an actor, Grossman, and his family, and the continued esteem of Goethe's mother, Wagner seems to have lived a happy existence in the later years. But they were destined to be fleeting ones. In a letter addressed to the Grossmans on March 1, 1779, Frau Rat Goethe expressed her concern because Wagner is so emaciated that he is nothing but skin and bones.[6] He died on March 4, 1779, only thirty-two years of age.

Since Wagner's reputation rests upon his dramas, we shall turn to them, paying special attention to the two most important ones, *Die Reue nach der Tat* and *Die Kindsmörderin*. Wagner's first play, *Der wohltätige Unbekannte* (1775), is a dramatization in one act of a popular anecdote told of Montesquieu. Showing the influence of Diderot and Mercier, Wagner unfolds scenes of great emotional intensity set in a realistic middle-class environment. The sentimental, lachrymose tone pervading the play is achieved by extolling a virtuous middle class which remains resolute in the face of wretched external circumstances. Mercier brought Wagner's play to the stage in Paris, and for a time it proved popular on both sides of the Rhine.

In the same year in which *Der wohltätige Unbekannte* appeared, Wagner wrote the dramatic farce *Prometheus, Deukalion, und die Rezensenten.* A witty harlequinade in "Knittelvers," it was devoted to a defense of Goethe's *Werther.* The detractors of Goethe are ridiculed in the manner of Goethe's puppet plays; instead of the author's using critics' names, small woodcuts immediately preceding the speeches identify the objects of the scathing attacks. Since many witticisms and idiomatic expressions are taken directly from Goethe's vocabulary, it is no small wonder that *Prometheus* was suspected, upon its appearance, to be a work of Goethe. This suspicion was all the more embarrassing to Goethe since the satirical farce contained several mischievous and indiscreet allusions to his efforts at obtaining a court appointment in Weimar. Goethe felt it necessary to issue a denial in the *Frankfurter Gelehrte Anzeigen* on April 9, 1775, to the effect that not he, but Heinrich Leopold Wagner was the author, and that he had written and published the work without his (Goethe's) knowledge.[7]

In the thinly veiled story around which Wagner builds his satire, Prometheus sends his son Deukalion into the world, and immediately the critics attack him with their senseless carping. They persecute genius with their hideous criticism and nip many a work of art in the bud. A clown introduces the sarcastic verses with a prologue and closes it with an epilogue written in Alsatian dialect in which he once more reproaches the reviewers. Although *Prometheus* is a lesser work of Wagner, it is a harbinger of dramas to come, revealing, as it does, the author's idiosyncrasies and his *modus operandi.* Already in this early satirical farce, Wagner's whole talent is imitative, and he achieves his best stylistic effect when reproducing the speech and mannerisms of those he knew; he has a penchant for the coarse expression and the sharp invective.

A malicious streak, coupled with an effort to enhance the

author's image, asserts itself in the dramatic dream satire in prose, *Voltaire am Abend seiner Apotheose* (1778). Wagner ridicules in rollicking manner the leader of the French Enlightenment, who shares with Wieland the scorn of the "Stürmer und Dränger." Borrowing heavily from Mercier's novel, *The Year 2440,* for his inspiration, Wagner has the vain poet, Voltaire, sink into a deathlike sleep after a successful performance of his drama, *Irene.* Thereupon the genius of the nineteenth century appears and hands the startled poet a dictionary from the year 1875. Turning it until he finds the entry under his name, Voltaire experiences bitter disappointment, for he is criticized for writing too prolifically. His dramas live on only in annotated textbook editions, and of the last one even the title has been lost. The once celebrated poet is easily accessible to the public in an anthology, *Esprit de Voltaire,* which contains, in two dainty duodecimo volumes, everything worthwhile written by the author. This revelation is too much for Voltaire, and at the end of the short drama he sinks back, uttering the words "Ah Dieux! Vous voulez donc me faire mourir."

Before turning to Wagner's two major dramatic works, it is important that we discuss his translation of Mercier's book on dramatic theory, *Du théâtre ou nouvel essai sur l'art dramatique* (1773), which appeared in 1776 under the title, *Neuer Versuch über die Schauspielkunst.* Several of the principles advocated by Mercier made a profound impression on Wagner and are incorporated in his two full-length dramas. Goethe and Lenz had been initially attracted to Mercier's book on its publication, and Goethe had originally contemplated a translation. When his enthusiasm for this undertaking flagged, he enlisted Wagner to carry out the project. The translation, completed, in essence, by the early part of 1775, is a faithful rendering from the French.

As mentioned in the chapter on Lenz, the Storm and Stress dramatists shared with Mercier his veneration for Shakespeare, his disdain for the three unities, and his reliance on "inner fire" rather than rules. In *Die Reue nach der Tat* and *Die Kindsmörderin,* Wagner follows the mode of writing established by Mercier and the young men of genius; but more than any other dramatist he is profoundly influenced by Mercier's tenet that the theater must be an instrument of social involvement. In his dramas, Wagner was to follow Mercier's precept that dramatic art must be enlarged so as to bring it close to everyday life and to focus on conditions which deserve exposure. According to Mercier, the dramatic scene is no longer reserved for a traditional portrayal of the conceited and unnatural personalities of the court, as is the case in the French Neo-Classical drama; rather, the true tragedy should concern itself with all strata of society, including the proletariat. The latter class, if interpreted correctly and sympathetically, can convey the tragic element in life far more poignantly and graphically than the kings in their stilted and outmoded language. It was ideas such as these, which Wagner encountered while translating Mercier, that were to have a telling effect on his own creations.

I   Die Reue nach der Tat

By basing *Die Reue nach der Tat* (1775) on actual events he witnessed in Strassburg and Saarbrücken, and by using realistic dialogue to depict true-to-life situations, Wagner followed the example of Herder, Goethe, Lenz, and Mercier, as opposed to the tradition of the French Classical theater. The division of the play into six acts, instead of the traditional five, seems to represent an additional effort to free the German drama from the shackles of French control. As was customary for poets who wrote dramas of a tendentious nature based on contemporary events, Wagner had his drama published anonymously. For a time Goethe or perhaps Lenz were suspected as the author.

Like Lenz in his major plays, Wagner develops his conflict from a basic antagonism between the aristocrats and the common people, more specifically from an utter disdain of the upper stratum toward their inferiors. In *Die Reue nach der Tat*, the aristocratic "Justizrätin" Langen thwarts her son's attempt to marry the daughter of a man of lower social station, the coachman Walz, and thereby brings about the tragic end of both young people. It matters not that, technically, mother Langen is not a member of the nobility but simply assumes her station through the prestigious title of her deceased husband; the important fact is that she identifies herself completely with the privileged group and acts accordingly. Like the Major's wife in *Der Hofmeister* she represents all too well the superficial, decadent society of her age.

Striving at all times to uphold her narrow-minded concept of honor and reputation, she is overly conscious of wearing the proper French bonnet, associating with socially acceptable people, and speaking in an overly refined language liberally sprinkled with French words. Once when she is returning from a drive with a Baroness she is irritated to see children of the lowest "Gsindel" play soldier in front of her house. Her annoyance changes to horror when she realizes that her nine-year-old son, Christian, is in command of this "Bagaschie."[8] Her irreverence for those of lower station extends to the obedient and capable governess of her daughter. In a fit of temper, she links the governess with "the rabble, of whom one can only expect to be annoyed."[9] Madam Langen is the foremost representative of the snobbish aristocracy, but the nobleman who, merely for diversion, directs an unsuspecting old Jew past the stable, to be mauled by a ferocious dog,[10] shows as well the callous disrespect of the privileged class for those considered inferior.

Madam Langen perpetuates her attitude toward the lower social stratum in her children. Her thirteen-year-old daughter, Caroline, the spoiled child of a doting parent, disobeys her governess in a most impertinent manner and begins to adopt the artificial and affected speech of her mother. On the other hand, her son Christian, who learns the proper aristocratic decorum from his mother, revolts against her precepts and looks up to his older brother, the aspiring attorney, as his model. The latter, in true Rousseauean fashion, puts a minimum of emphasis on book learning and instead insists that the boy teach himself by relying on his emotions and his intuitive nature for guidance. To quote "Assessor" Langen, "[Ein Genie] hat sich immer von selbst gebildet"[11] ("A genius has always educated himself"). From this we are to infer that Christian's association with the children of the underprivileged classes, who are untainted by civilization, is a positive molding influence in the boy's program of self-education. There is no doubt that Wagner consciously incorporated a pedagogical message into the drama, and in order to give his theories relevance, carefully constructed the locale of several children. By providing intimate glimpses of the environment, speech, and mannerisms of Caroline and Christian Langen and Lenchen Walz, he, interestingly enough, also brought to the German stage children who are alive and real. They represent progression from the artificial paper creations of Gerstenberg's *Ugolino* and of Lessing's *Miss Sara Sampson.*

It is not the children, however, who are the principals of the drama and enlist our sympathy, but rather "Assessor" Langen and Fridericke Walz, two young people who are of the same age and spirit as the "Stürmer und Dränger." Like Wagner, Langen is interested in writing but has decided, for practical reasons, to follow a career in law, which he studied at the university. His profession never seriously enters into the action, although he receives an appointment as state attorney just before the play's final crisis. At the outset of the play, Langen appears to us as a sensitive young man of feeling who is completely absorbed in tracing a silhouette of Fridericke, with whom he is deeply in love. In busying himself with a likeness of his beloved, he reminds us of the Prince in *Emilia Galotti* and of Goethe's Werther. His wildly throbbing heart, which he can feel in his very finger tips, almost prevents him from accomplishing his task and reveals a young man who is completely guided by his emotions. Goethe's and Lavater's preoccupation with physiognomy has left its mark on Wagner, for Langen analyzes Fridericke's character from the profile of her silhouette for his friend Werner. Pointing to the silhouette, he says:

Do you see this high, softly rounded forehead; the true ideal of gentility and affection: heavenly peace seems to hover over it:—This almost unnoticeable transition to the nose, how much equanimity and solidity of character it expresses![12]

The detailed and convincing scenes of family life in the Langen home, supplemented by copious stage directions, seem to anticipate the methods of Naturalism at the end of the nineteenth century. Unfortunately, after the middle of Act III the realistic dialogue gives way to stilted speech, and the actions of the characters, especially of Langen and his mother, become arbitrary and are no longer causally related to the environment and social determinants which the author depicted so carefully at the outset of the drama.

In portraying the milieu, the everyday life, and the motivations of the lower-middle-class family, the Walzes, Wagner follows the same pattern as with their aristocratic counterparts; and he encounters the same pitfalls. When we meet the coachman Walz initially in Act II, he is the upright but coarse-grained burgher whose every action and utterance seems to reflect his occupational status. He is a vigorous, gruff, hotheaded, yet likable man, an old soldier, who served Prussia in the war and is both fond and proud of his daughters. His speech is pithy, replete with proverbs, and spiced with Alsatian idioms. He like to use "gafflich"[13] ("nosy") "Fickeltäten"[14] ("problems") "Mumenten" ("moments") "verschammiert" ("enthralled") and the Gallicized expression, "wenn's beliebt"[15] ("if you please"). Like Götz and his entourage, Walz speaks the turbulent, rough-and-ready language of the "Kraftkerls." A case in point is his conversation with his daughter, Fridercke, where he questions Langen's intensions toward her by saying:

Halts Maul, du Bohnenstange, du Wachspüppchen! weist den Henker, was ihm all schon in Sinn gekommen ist. Sapperment! hat er dich nicht wollen desertieren machen, he! meinst ich weiss es nicht?—Drum wusst ich nicht, warum der Kerl vor so da sass, als hätt er Teufelsdreck gefressen . . .[16]

Shut up, you bean pole, you wax doll! God knows what all got into his mind. Dammit! Didn't he want to desert you, eh? Do you think I don't know. Didn't I know why the rascal sat here as if he had eaten the devil's excrement.

The bombastic tone, the short ejaculatory expressions, the coarse epithets, and the profane word "Sapperment" are typical of the passionate and virile speech of genius.

Wagner gives the scenes constructed around the coachman Walz color and authenticity by linking them with reminiscences of his experiences at the Günderode's in Saarbrücken. Karl, hired as a groom by Walz, had formerly served a Chancellor who was forced to sell horse and carriage. Karl wept at his departure, for all the servants had been treated like children. That the Chancellor is a thinly veiled allusion to Günderode is obvious. When Karl further relates that the Chancellor lost his property, ruined his health, and was persecuted by the ruling Count, Walz replies that such is often one's lot at the small courts; that "not every ruler is an Emperor Joseph, nor every Queen a Theresia."[17] This glorification of the reigning monarch, repeated later in the drama, causes one to suspect that Wagner hoped for royal favor, maybe in the form of a position in a legation.[18]

When the effervescent Walz, bubbling over with bourgeois pride, consents to the engagement and marriage of his daughter to Langen, the stage is set for a dramatic confrontation between the two families, since we know that Langen's mother is opposed to such a union. But no two-sided conflict develops. Without warning or motivation, mother Langen changes from a peevish snob into a raging "Machtweib," has the Queen put Fridericke in a convent and her son in confinement, and the conflict is over. When Langen, pining away for Fridericke, becomes mortally ill and loses his mind, the mother "rues her deed" (hence the title) and consents to the marriage after all. But it is too late—Fridericke has taken poison the day before she is released and dies in Langen's arms, whereupon Langen rushes into the adjoining room and commits suicide.

Langen and Fridericke, who should be the two main personages of the play, are mere puppets, moving according to the whim of Langen's mother and the author. After the first scene of the play, there are no episodes which show Langen as a convincing representative of his upper-middle-class environment; and at no time is he cognizant of being caught between two powerful conflicting social forces, which his love for a girl of lower rank might occasion. Rather, he regards his callous, obstinate mother as his only obstacle, but offers no resistance to her dictates. Here, then, is a weakness inherent in the drama. Instead of having the two lovers caught relentlessly in a web of social determinants, they are merely victims of a malicious woman's intrigue. In true Werther fashion, Langen's sensitive nature, deeply wronged, seeks refuge in extravagant sentimental and emotional effusions, which finally culminate in mad delirium.

Fridericke is an equally passive and colorless individual, who has inherited none of her father's originality and flamboyance. In the tradition of *Miss Sara Sampson* and her English counterparts in the middle-class drama, Fridericke is a virtuous, sentimental young maiden in love with her suitor, but never demoniacally obsessed by her feeling for him. Wagner valiantly attempts to have her reflect some of the naïve and intuitive innocence of Gretchen when she tells her father of her feeling for Langen: "I loved him before I myself knew that I wanted to love him."[19] But this unconscious attraction for Langen is not convincing because in the next episode Fridericke decides quite rationally that she must break off relations with her lover because of an old folk superstition. The maltreated Jewish peddler, who comes to the Walz's for medication, relates to Fridericke that he is an accursed man, who lost his wife at childbirth, and in his abject poverty has had to care for their crippled son for sixty years—all because he married against his father's wishes and was cursed for it. Fridericke, quick to see the parallels to her own life, does not want the curse of Langen's mother on her head, and out of the strength of superstitious belief is willing to renounce her love. When Fridericke learns, although mistakenly, that Langen's mother favors the marriage after all, she can love as passionately as before.

In contrast to Langen and Fridericke, some of the minor characters are authentic creations whose speech and actions reflect their social background and cultural heritage. The old Jew, who displays his pack of dry goods and notions in the Walz home and speaks his distinctive dialect, is taken from real life. In like manner, the French governess in the Langen household, wrestling with the spoiled brats and the German grammar and syntax, seems to be an individual that Wagner personally observed. In the following passage she complains to Langen's friend, Werner, about her frustrating attempts to teach Caroline accepted social manners:

Sie ahb gesehn, wie ein abominable Gang sie at; kann sie nit mal mahk ein Reverenz, die Olzbock; und malgre tout cela is sie die Favorite ihrer Mutter; sahkt man denn etwas, so at man des Enkers Dank davor. (*Caroline weint laut, die Mutter tröstet sie.*) Schreit sie nit wie ein Kalb! will jetzt die Mutter ahb, sie soll schweick, muss sie ihr wieder verspreck was Neues.[20]

You have seen what an abominable gait she has. She can't even curtsy, the clumsy ox; and in spite of all she is her mother's darling. If one says something contrary, one really gets chewed out. (*Caroline cries loudly and her mother comforts her.*) Doesn't she bleat like a calf! If her mother wants her to be quiet, she must promise her something anew.

But in these individualized characterizations Wagner has not learned to portray complex, modern characters in the manner of Lenz. Using the traditional polarity, he depicts only those who enlist all our sympathy or their opposites whom we are to detest wholeheartedly. In throwing overboard the three unities, he likewise fails to realize the true dramatic potential which Lenz was able to exploit by disregarding the confines of time, place, and action and fashioning multiple realistic, episodic structures in their stead. Wagner still feels himself so bound by the traditional French limitation of place that the whole action takes place in the Langen home, the Walz home, and a public square downtown. In *Die Reue nach der Tat* Wagner could have made the singular episodes more vivid by staging them in their actual setting rather than by having the characters statically describe such events. For instance, a poignant scene in the convent, graphically illustrating Fridericke's plight, would have been more effective than having Walz simply relate his visit to his daughter; or an episode actually showing Langen suffering in detention would have been more vivid than little Christian's description of his brother's delirium. The frequent stage entrances and exits deliberately violate the rules of the French Classical theater, although all too often this movement of characters serves no real purpose.

Wagner violates the unity of time by having the action of the play cover a period of several weeks. Here again the time span fulfills no essential function. It is not used to reinforce the element of social determinism, as in Lenz's plays, nor to show a development in character. All that transpires about the three weeks that Langen is confined is that he deteriorates physically and mentally, and his friends suffer insomnia worrying about him.[21]

However, by enlisting sympathy for Langen and Fridericke on the part of Langen's brother Christian, his friend Werner, and Walz, Wagner is able to create dramatic tension; for through the reactions of the friends the audience, too, becomes involved in the efforts of the two young lovers to be united. When, at the end of Act IV, Werner reports that Langen's mother has changed her mind, we are prepared for a peaceful solution of the conflict between mother and son. But the emotional intensity reaches new heights when Langen, Werner, and Walz realize that the mother had merely planned a malicious ruse; she is only intent on shifting the onus of blame from herself to the officers of the Queen by having the latter place Langen in detention and Fridericke in a convent. Werner's outrage knows no bounds, and the colorful Walz explodes with fiery expletives and coarse invectives when they become aware of the sorry plight of the two principals, brought on by the mother's cruel intrigues. The last scene, ending in the death of the young lovers and the remorse of the mother, is packed with the effusive emotion which made the drama popular and theatrically effective in a sentimental age. The leading actor of that age, Friedrich Ludwig Schröder, played the part of Walz on the Hamburg stage, and the Seyler troupe and the Mannheim Theater included *Die Reue nach der Tat* in their repertory soon after the drama appeared.

Sometimes, in an effort to shock and impress his audience, Wagner lets his Storm and Stress exuberance get the better of him and resorts to wild tirades which are overly bombastic, crass in effect, and generally in bad taste. For instance, Werner, thoroughly frustrated in his efforts to help his friend Langen, vents his spleen at a poor woman who innocently offers to pray for him in exchange for alms for herself and her children. Werner is so incensed that he says: "One should choke you and rip out your breasts with glowing tongs and fill the holes with pitch and sulphur; and you want to pray for me?—for you! for you!"[22] Langen, in his disturbed state, toward the close of the drama, likewise uses offensive language and ill-chosen images. He addresses Walz thusly: "Out with you, you old mustache, hair for hair I'll tear it out . . . come, be my father too, and beat my brains out and prop your mustache on them."[23] In using crudities of this type to express pent-up emotions, Wagner may have imitated the bombastic drama of the Silesian baroque and the most flagrant excesses found in Shakespearean plays. But in the last analysis outside influences are not to be blamed as much as Wagner's personal predilection for including bizarre, off-color elements in his literary works. And yet this play, with all its deficiencies, is an important milestone which the German revolutionary drama had to pass in its effort to leave behind the vestiges of a barren, pseudo-Classical French-oriented theater in search of a more vital one, where man with heart and emotion confronted contemporary problems in realistic surroundings. Wagner's next play, *Die Kindsmörderin,* represented another step forward.

II Die Kindsmörderin

Of all the dramatists of the Storm and Stress period no one approaches Wagner in *Die Kindsmörderin* in anticipating techniques of "konsequenter" or consistent realism, which were in vogue in Germany over a century later. In giving us a slice of real life in which individuals appear no longer as sketchy types or caricatures, but as clearly delineated, genuine human beings, Wagner surpasses Lenz's *Der Hofmeister* and *Die Soldaten* and Goethe's *Clavigo*. His characters express themselves in a popular idiom, liberally sprinkled with coarse and dialectal expressions, to give their dialogue a forceful actuality. Supplemented by copious stage directions, the action is depicted in all its unvarnished and natural starkness. Like the Naturalists, Wagner prefers as well to show the sordid side of life and to enlist sympathy for the lower social strata.

Again, as in *Die Reue nach der Tat* and Lenz's major dramas, the dramatic conflict in *Die Kindsmörderin* arises from a basic clash between two strata of society. On the one hand, the aristocracy shows a callous disrespect for the middle class; on the other, the burghers have become suspect of the irresponsible caprices of the upper class, even though they are still flattered by their condescension. Here is a résumé of the plot: Lieutenant von Gröningseck, an aristocratic officer quartered in the home of the butcher Martin Humbrecht, for devious ulterior motives has invited Humbrecht's wife and eighteen-year-old daughter, Evchen, to a carnival ball. To cap off the festivities, Gröningseck suggests that all three go to an inn, The Yellow Cross, for breakfast. In the inn, which is actually a brothel, Gröningseck has rented two dingy rooms, and after serving both women intoxicants and the mother a sleeping potion as well, he seduces Evchen. When Evchen immediately regrets her conduct and reproaches her escort for violating her, Gröningseck promises to make amends by marrying her in five months, when he will come of age. Evchen consents to his proposal. She is, of course, immediately pregnant and spends most of her time trying to keep the news from her proud parents. Gröningseck, who actually wants to keep his bargain, has his good intentions thwarted by an officer friend, Lieutenant Hasenpoth. The latter forges a letter to Evchen in which Gröningseck states that he has no interest in her and that she shall give the expected child to a foundling hospital. Distraught, Evchen leaves home, finds refuge with a poor washerwoman, where she gives birth. Driven to madness by her desperate state, she kills the child. Too late her father forgives her, and

Gröningseck learns about his friend's malicious ruse. At the end of the drama, officers take Evchen into custody on a murder charge.

Schneider lists Act I among the best creations that dramas of this period have to offer.[24] By virtue of its concentrated dramatic impact it is theatrically effective, and its wealth of realistic detail is skillfully blended into the action and plays a very relevant part in influencing Evchen's behavior. We are not to believe, as in the traditional drama, that Evchen suffered a moral lapse, but that social and environmental factors, too powerful for her to overcome, determined her fall. To begin with, Gröningseck, as a member of the privileged officer corps, has been at this inn before and is experienced in methods of inducing gullible burgher maidens of the town to submit to his wishes. By flattering the good-natured but vain and foolish mother, he not only gains her favor, but kindles a spark of jealousy in the daughter, thus making the latter more receptive to him. The shabbily furnished rooms of the inn and the people who attend to them, such as the repulsive landlady and the dissolute maid, Marianel, likewise contribute to an atmosphere where Evchen's resistance breaks down. Even the carefully described ball clothes, the masks, and Gröningseck's risqué stories are factors that cannot be overlooked.

Although *Die Kindsmörderin* was published by Schwickert in Leipzig (anonymously) in 1776, censors took offense at the crude and sordid elements in the opening act and forbade it to be played. A revised version by Karl Lessing, in which Act I was deleted entirely, was produced on the stage in the following year. Lessing's revision induced Wagner to rewrite the drama in 1779;[25] here again the opening scene in the inn was omitted. Although these later versions were allowed to be performed, they never met with stage success and lacked the intrinsic unity of the original. In the form of the anonymous publication of 1776, *Die Kindsmörderin* enjoyed a renascence on the German stage at the beginning of the twentieth century,[26] despite the fact that an influential critic such as Hettner still found fault with "the terrible first act ... and the unspeakable crudities and elements of bad taste."[27] That we evaluate differently today is born out by Schneider's praise of the opening scene mentioned above, and by a casual perusal of recent theater repertories, which reveals that this drama is played on the leading stages in post-World War II Germany.

While Evchen's seduction is the central event of the opening act, Act II begins to unfold the consequences from the standpoint of the young girl. By depicting, in close detail, her home environment, Wagner shows how strongly the social pressures—here in the guise of family tradition—determine her future course of action. The central figure who determines and upholds the mores of the household is the father, Martin Humbrecht. Following in the tradition of Lessing's Odoardo, Lenz's Wesener, and Wagner's Walz, he is the upright, honest, and proud burgher who lives strictly according to the custom of his class, tolerates no innovations, and distrusts the aristocrats. He is a blustery, narrow-minded, puritanical tyrant with a choleric temperament who terrifies his family. On hearing that his wife and daughter have attended the ball, he says:

Lasst die immerhin drauf herumtänzeln, die drauf gehören, wer wehrt's ihnen?—für die vornehmen Herren und Damen, Junker und Fräuleins, die vor lauter Vornehmigkeit nicht wissen, wo sie mit des lieben Herrgotts seiner Zeit hin sollen, für die mag es ein ganz artigs Vergnügen sein; wer hat was darwider?—Aber Handwerksweiber, Bürgerstöchter sollen die Nas' davon lassen; die können auf Hochzeiten, Meisterstückschmäusen, und was des Zeugs mehr ist, Schuh' genug zerschleifen, brauchen nicht noch ihre Ehr' und guten Namen mit auf's Spiel zu setzen—Wenn denn vollends ein zuckersüsses Bürschchen in der Uniform oder ein Barönchen, des sich Gott erbarm! ein Mädchen vom Mittelstand an solche örter hinführt, so ist zehn gegen eins zu verwetten, dass er sie nicht wieder nach Haus bringt, wie er sie abgeholt hat.[28]

Let those dance about there who belong there, who will deny them the privilege? For the aristocratic ladies and gentlemen, landowners and noblewomen, who, because of their high rank do not know how to while away the time that God has given them, for them it may be a very pleasant diversion. Who objects? But wives of artisans and daughters of the middle class should steer clear of it; they can wear out enough shoes at weddings, at banquets of the guilds, and the like, and need not place their honor and good name in jeopardy. When, however, a sweet lad in uniform or a Baron, may God have mercy, takes a girl from the middle class to such places, then it is ten against one that he will not bring her home as she was when they started out.

Humbrecht's style, compared to that of his literary forebears, is much more closely tuned to the actual, everyday speech of his social class. Containing coarse, popular idiom liberally spiced with humor, ridicule, and irony, his language reflects a colorful, flamboyant personality. Humbrecht's visual image, delineated clearly in the stage directions, complements his speech; when he appears in the morning wearing his night doublet (*Nachtkamisöl-chen*), sleeping cap, and shoes worn at the heels,[29] he is again an original creation representing the inhabitants in the back alleys of Strassburg. Worthy of comment is the fact that, in many ways, Humbrecht is a precursor of the character of Hebbel's Meister Anton; nowhere is this more evident than at the end of the drama where, dealt a shattering blow, he rips open his jacket buttons, takes a deep breath, and exclaims: "The whole world is getting too small for me."[30]

As the daughter of such a forceful activist, Evchen must embark on a course of action but proceeds with extreme caution. Reared to observe a strict moral code and to obey her parents, she exemplifies a virtuous young lady of the eighteenth century. In the seduction episode she reminds us originally of Richardson's Clarissa. Lovelace, the ideal libertine, lures Clarissa into a house of ill fame, and seduces her while she is under the influence of narcotics. The similarity to Wagner's story is readily apparent. But in her home Evchen becomes a typical burgher maiden of the German sentimental age, reads novels and Young's *Night Thoughts,* and, except for indulging in a few emotional tirades in the Storm and Stress style, remains quite passive in her feelings and actions. She fears her father, but is hopeful that her quiet virtue and Gröningseck's promise of marriage will enable her somehow to surmount her problems. Only when Evchen realizes that her lover has betrayed her does she resort to action; and as we shall see later, her subsequent fate reminds one strongly of Gretchen's experiences.

It would seem, at first glance, that through the personage of Gröningseck Wagner wants to effect a rapprochement between the two hostile classes; that Wagner believes that true, unselfish love can overcome the inbred evils of parasitism and victimization which are so rampant in an ostensibly civilized society. But a meliorist solution is not forthcoming because society as a whole is not ready for it and because Gröningseck as an individual is not strong enough to bring it about. Gröningseck belongs to the unstable sentimentalists whose good intentions never reach fruition. Mellefont, the Prince of Guastalla, Weislingen, and Clavigo are his forebears. Like Lessing's Prince and Goethe's Clavigo, he is under the evil influence of a stronger friend. As a sensual, hedonistic young aristocrat who regards burgher maidens as fair game, he callously plans the conquest of Evchen, only to suffer pangs of conscience afterward. Impressed by her moral goodness, which separates her from the burgher girls who resist weakly but nevertheless are flattered by the love of an aristocratic officer, the softhearted Gröningseck has compassion for Evchen. For the most part, though, he is merely interested in creating the illusion of being genuinely concerned. For instance, he asks the schoolmaster cousin of Humbrecht to express to Evchen his best wishes and sincere desire to be at her service, "if only for the sake of politeness."[31]

If Gröningseck is vacillating and even, at times, compassionate toward the middle class, his friend and evil genius, Hasenpoth, has nothing but contempt for the lower strata. Reared to believe that those below him exist only for his sport, he will go to any lengths to preserve social segregation. Demonstrating some of the ruthlessness and treachery of Lessing's Marinelli, he coldly and rationally devises the plan of the forged letters to effectively seal Evchen's doom. Ironically enough, Hasenpoth's attitude reflects typical Storm and Stress views. Even though the dramatists of the period enlisted sympathy for the victims of misalliance, they felt that the barriers between the two classes were too difficult to surmount and that interclass marriages could only be disastrous.

When Evchen receives Gröningseck's forged letter, she feels compelled to act. As a remarkably modern character who cannot communicate with her father, her mother, or her suitor, and is rejected by the latter, she feels completely isolated, leaves home, and finds refuge outside accepted society in the home of a poor washerwoman. By means of language, mood, and minute description, Wagner depicts the sordid, wretched living conditions which coincide with Evchen's frame of mind. When the washerwoman relates ugly rumors about butcher Humbrecht's daughter, whose actions have caused the mother to die of a broken heart and the father to put a price of one hundred Thaler on her head for information about her whereabouts, Evchen admits her identity and begs her benefactress to collect the money. The victim of fate, Evchen has decided almost existentially on a course of action. She no longer displays the passivity of an Emilia Galotti or a Fräulein von Sternheim, but instead demonstrates— although in vain—a certain emotive and moral vigor. Ultimately, utter despair wears her down to the point where she loses her senses; and in a fit of madness she kills her newborn child.

Putting into practice Mercier's tenet that drama should treat all classes of society, including the lowest, Wagner begins a new innovation for the German theater by having a motley group of base and shabby people enter into the action of *Die Kindsmör- derin*. Besides the washerwoman and the hotel maid, Marianel, mentioned above, there are Lissel, Evchen's maid, and the two jailers (*Fausthammer*). The latter offend by their coarse, insen- sitive manner while delivering Humbrecht's wife's stolen snuffbox and subsequently investigating Evchen's disappearance from home. The jailers' language is most striking, since they speak in pure dialect, bringing to mind the speech of Hauptmann's char- acters in the 1890's. Quoted below is the conversation between the two men, when, smelling some extra wages, they fix in their mind Evchen's marks of identification which they will need to find her :

ERSTER FAUSTHAMMER: Gottlob! do gitt's doch widder a paar sechs schilli Biesslä ze verdienä!
ZWEITER FAUSTHAMMER: Vergiss jetzt widder d'Kunsign, häscht's g'hört!
ERSTER FAUSTHAMMER: Dreck uf dien Nas. I waiss gewiss nimmi?— a Bunne rung, nun a Mantel mit brunem Bodä, unn—unn—o's ist mer z'inn, ich seh sie schunn.[32]

FIRST JAILER: God be praised, here we can earn a few six shilling pieces.
SECOND JAILER: Now forget the marks of identification again, you hear!
FIRST JAILER: Go to hell! You think I don't know—a round bonnet, a coat of brown background, and, and, I remember all right, I see her already.

In the dialogue above an attempt is made to reproduce exact speech patterns. Previously Wagner, as well as Lenz, had the lower classes speak normal stage language interspersed only on occasions with dialectal or colloquial terms.

Now that we have discussed the significant aspects of the drama, it will be interesting to determine to what extent Wagner showed independence and to what degree he imitated other writers. Since we know that Goethe accused Wagner of plagiarism for using the Gretchen theme in *Die Kindsmörderin,* it will be fruitful to see just how much Wagner is indebted to an episode in the early *Faust* version. Evchen, like Gretchen, is seduced by a young man with an evil companion as an accomplice, who helps, among other things, to provide a sleeping potion for the girl's mother. Evchen, too, is visibly shaken by idle gossip about a girl who has been led astray, just as Gretchen is in the Well scene. Both protagonists are bothered by their evil conscience in church, and both murder their illegitimate child. Mentally disturbed, both sing an Ophelia-type song. In each instance they are to be executed for their sins. It goes without saying that there are also strong differences between Goethe's and Wagner's dramas. While Wagner wrote primarily a tendentious play of contemporary topical interest, Goethe fashioned his Gretchen episode into a timeless love story which represents a significant phase in Faust's titanic struggle to fathom the essence of life.

While the Goethean influence is undeniable, it may be that Lenz's dramas had more impact on *Die Kindsmörderin* than did *Faust.* The Major of *Der Hofmeister,* in his coarse-mannered but tender-hearted relation to Gustchen, seems to be mirrored in the character of Humbrecht. Like Gustchen, Evchen finds refuge in her pregnant condition in a remote hut, where she is the guest of a poor woman named Martha. But there are even more similarities to *Die Soldaten.* Both the latter drama and *Die Kindsmörderin* are social protests against the fickle, irresponsible officer corps, who victimize the daughters of the middle class. Both have a Strassburg locale as a background, with historical events, local gossip, and authentic characters forming the basis of the central action. It is especially one episode in Act III of *Die Kindsmörderin* that reminds one strongly of *Die Soldaten*: Major Lindsthal, calling at Gröningseck's room to inform him that his furlough has been approved, relates an incident that took place in an officers' saloon the day before.[33] The details of a scandal involving card playing, gambling, cheating, and officer's honor are not important, except as they throw light on the pitfalls of officers' life caused by a bored and unnatural existence. Like Lenz in his

Coffee House scene, Wagner seeks to show that the officers, leading a dull, frustrated life, indulge in a variety of pastimes, often at the expense of the lower classes. However, while Lenz's Coffee House encounter is simply one of a series of episodes which helps us to understand why officers behave as they do, Major Lindsthal's description of life in the saloon is an isolated, secondhand account of group decorum, serves no real purpose, and represents the one and only glaring irrelevancy in the drama. In summary, the Lindsthal episode serves to show how Wagner was led astray by imitating Lenz. Wagner was no innovator in dramatic structure, nor in the skillful use of language or pantomime to characterize personages, as was Lenz; and where Lenz's characters display psychological depth and a cynical approach to the world's ills, Wagner's personages remain on a superficial level, striving positively to point out and eradicate certain contemporary social evils.

Wagner's drama is a plea for lightening the sentence of a mother guilty of infanticide, and consequently, for removal of the death penalty. It sympathizes with a girl of good character who has been forced, by a corrupt society, to commit a crime. In this respect, the drama reflects a Rousseauean spirit, and it is especially Master Humbrecht, the butcher's cousin, who stands for Rousseauean integrity, advocating a return to man's unadulterated nature. As mentioned previously, the aristocratic officers are chastised for their parasitic inclinations, but the middle class does not go unscathed. Mother Humbrecht is taken to task for falling prey to the flattery of an officer because of her vanity and foolhardiness, and the harsh, quick-tempered father carries his share of the blame because of his false sense of honor. Furthermore, Wagner finds fault with the mechanical severity of laws which tolerate no exceptions; through Gröningseck he condemns the "criminal insensibility"[34] of the officers of the court.

Vitally related to the cruel fate of Evchen, these tendentious elements are well integrated into the action of the drama and help to give the play unity of tone. An austere construction likewise serves to render the drama effective and stageworthy. Paying only lip service to the Storm and Stress flaunting of the three unities, Wagner still adopts in *Die Kindsmörderin* a conservative, traditional framework. Except for the introductory scene in the inn and the final one in Frau Martha's house, all the action is concentrated in the Humbrecht home. For obvious reasons the time that elapses is nine months, which allows Wagner to show dramatically the salient cause-and-effect elements of the seduction. The number of characters is limited to a baker's dozen, and except for the Major Lindsthal episode, all the action contributes to the unity of the story.

By minutely depicting the petty foibles of aristocracy and bourgeoisie, the inane class prejudices and their consequences, Wagner portrays life realistically, exactly as it might have happened. His dialogue and speech pattern are more genuine than those of other "Stürmer und Dränger" and compare with the language used later by the Naturalists. Indeed, it is to the fact that Wagner was a precursor of later literary movements that he owes his significance today. In the liberal and effective use of dialect he anticipated many writers of the nineteenth and twentieth centuries. Like Lenz, Wagner was a forerunner of Büchner and of modern dramatists, when he found his poetic inspiration in the shabby existence of the lower classes. Like Brecht and his school, Wagner wrote his dramas with a message. The poignancy of the theme of *Die Kindsmörderin* still makes the drama stageworthy today, even though this play reveals an author whose dramatic talent was shallower, more observational, and more conventional than that of Lenz.

CHAPTER 4

Maler Müller:
A Painter-Poet of the Palatinate

AN IMPORTANT member of the Storm and Stress group was Johann Friedrich Müller, who preferred to call himself "Maler Müller"; for besides being a dramatist, he achieved a reputation as a designer, etcher, and painter. He has often been called the Romanticist among the dramatists of the age of genius—not without justification, since he treated themes which have been transmitted to us through "Volksbücher," and since he interspersed his loosely constructed prose dramas with verse and lyrical interludes. To a certain extent, he achieved the Romantic ideal of uniting and synthesizing all the arts; yet his artistic spirit is firmly linked with the Storm and Stress. Like Lenz and Wagner, he depicted a realistic middle-class milieu, replete with sensual, coarse, and crass elements. But his dramas also form a bridge to those of the two dramatists who will be treated subsequently in this study: Klinger and Leisewitz. Like the latter men, Müller created youthful heroes who revolt not so much against a particular segment of society as against the whole world order, which prevents them from reaching their true potential. In their frustrations, these heroes generate fierce pathological passions which, in turn, buoy them up and guide them intuitively.

Maler Müller was born on January 13, 1749, at Kreuznach in the Palatinate. His father, who was alternately a baker, brewer, cooper, and innkeeper, died when the boy was eleven; and the dire financial straits which ensued forced him to interrupt his schooling in 1763. At home he evinced a talent for painting, and in 1766 he was sent to Zweibrücken to be apprenticed to the painter at the ducal court, Konrad Manlich. Here he remained for eight years, having impressed his patron with his growing artistic ability. In the meantime, he read avidly, became an enthusiastic admirer of Klopstock and the Göttingen "Bund," and began to write poems, one of which was forwarded to Klopstock and published in the Göttingen *Musenalmanach*.[1] In his last year in Zweibrücken, Müller had a torrid love affair with Charlotte Kärner, the daughter of the local superintendent. Whether career conflicts, the objections of Lottchen's father, mutual incompatibility, or a combination of several factors caused Müller to break relations with "das braune Fräulein," we do not know. At any rate, she bore him a child and became the inspiration for poems, idylls, and dramatic figures. As we shall see later, the heroine of the drama *Golo und Genoveva* resembles Charlotte. Through the figure of Golo, Müller expresses the remorse and guilt feeling which he experienced on forsaking his beloved.

Since the Charlotte episode dictated that Müller leave his familiar surroundings, he moved in 1774 to Mannheim, where his reputation as a painter helped him to meet influential men in the world of art as well as literature. In 1775 he initiated a friendship with Christian Friedrich Schubart, then a disciple of Klopstock and the Göttingen school, but later a revolutionary of the Storm and Stress mold. Schubart published some of Müller's poems in his journal, *Deutsche Chronik*. Sometimes before February 5, 1775, Müller made Goethe's acquaintance in Mannheim and visited him later in Frankfurt, although, ironically, Goethe was not interested in the poet, but in the painter.[2] In the following year, H. L. Wagner, on a trip from Frankfurt to Strassburg, called on Müller, and at this time Müller also met Lenz and Klinger.[3] Müller carried on a correspondence with the Storm and Stress dramatists, but unfortunately only a few of these letters have been preserved. In a letter from Lenz to Müller dated April 16, 1776, Lenz intimates that the two writers exchanged their works, for Lenz assumes that Müller has already received *Die Soldaten* and asks for a copy of *Golo*.[4] Müller's important dramas were written, or at least begun, during this period, though they were published only many years later. Apart from the nucleus of Storm and Stress writers Müller was also well acquainted with Wieland and Lessing; the former he met in 1777 during Wieland's sojourn in Mannheim, and the latter in the same town where the mutual friends exerted their efforts toward establishing a National theater.

Müller still considered himself a painter by profession, and in 1778 he left Mannheim, supported by a court stipend and a subscription (in the raising of which Goethe had taken a prominent part) in order to continue his art studies in Rome. He was not to return to Germany. His artistic ambitions were never realized, either in painting or in writing, although he continued to have a devoted following and acted as unofficial host to the many German esthetes who, over the years, made pilgrimages to Rome. He died there in 1825.

When Müller went to Rome, he had already established a reputation as a writer of idylls in rhythmic prose. Strongly influenced by Gessner's works, his *Der erschlagene Abel* (1775) and *Adams erstes Erwachen und erste selige Nächte* (1778) still sing of an ideal, primitive life in sentimental fashion, but the realistically depicted nature moods and the frequent outburts of passion unmistakably reveal Storm and Stress tendencies. A syntax exhibiting inversions, anacolutha, and a host of interjections also points to a new mode popularized by Lavater and Klinger. The tendency to forsake the dainty pastoral landscape painting in favor of a more robust depiction of nature is even more evident in Müller's Palatine idylls, *Die Schafschur* (1775) and *Das Nusskernen*, written a little later, but first published in 1811. In the latter creations, we meet the simple country folk in a natural setting, speaking a dialectally flavored idiom and singing folk songs of the area. Based on exact observation of peasant life in the Kreuznach and Zweibrücken area, these stories employ a course, unvarnished language, reminiscent of Wagner. In *Das Nusskernen*, the popular Storm and Stress theme of the seduction of a simple girl and her subsequent execution for infanticide forms an integral part of the story. In this case, the sad plight of the girl is used as a vehicle for registering the social protest of the young generation against the heartless elders and society's rigid laws.

Less satisfying artistically are Müller's pseudo-Classical idylls, *Der Satyr Mopsus* (1775), *Bacchidon und Milon* (1775) and *Der Faun Molon*.[5] Dressed in garments of antiquity, the characters in these stories appear as hybrid creatures who speak, for the most part, in the crass, vigorous tone of the "Kraftkerls," only to express themselves, now and then, in gallant Rococo phrases that seem totally out of place. The trappings of antiquity are merely a flimsy disguise of persons and social conditions in the poet's Palatine home which he wants to satirize.

The two Palatine idylls and *Bacchidon und Milon* are written in dialogue, thus containing rudimentary elements of dramatic form. In the company of Goethe and his fellow "Stürmer und Dränger," Müller was attracted to the genre of the drama, although his epically oriented talents and his inability to fathom the requirements of the stage prevented his achieving real success in this art form. His two best known dramas, *Fausts Leben dramatisiert* and *Golo und Genoveva* were both begun in 1775–76, in the period when Müller was drawn into Goethe's orbit.

I   Faust

On approaching a study of Müller's dramatic creations based on the Faust legend, the first question that naturally comes to mind is the one concerning the author's indebtedness to Goethe for poetic inspiration and treatment of theme. In the preface to *Fausts Leben,* Müller claims that when he began to write his drama he did not know of Goethe's and Lessing's plans to treat the same subject.[6] Two leading Müller's scholars see no reason to doubt this assertion, although they readily admit that the Faust theme and its new interpretation was a popular one among the young geniuses of the 1770's.[7] Insofar as these poets received their impetus and direction from Goethe, Müller, too, was influenced by the acknowledged leader.

In the preface to *Fausts Leben,* Müller outlines his concept of the hero as a sort of composite of Goethe's Prometheus and Klinger's Kraftkerl:

A fellow who felt all his strength and likewise the curb which chance and fate laid upon him, and which he wished to cast off—one who seeks ways and means, who has the courage to suppress everything that bars his way and seeks to hinder him—one who has warmth enough in his breast to link himself to a devil who approaches him in a spirit of sincerity and confidence.[8]

Müller envisions a great individualist in the Storm and Stress tradition who revolts against convention and tradition to the extent that he will condone ruthlessness and excess to realize his full potential.

Originally Müller planned *Faust* as a monumental work in five parts. *Fausts Leben* represents the first of these, and the *Situation aus Fausts Leben* an important element of the second. Since the *Situation* episode was printed first (Mannheim 1776), and since the characters of Faust and Mephisto as developed here form the basis for all later sequels, we will turn our attention to this fragment first. Consisting of two scenes which depict the dramatic climax and turning point of Faust's life, the short *Situation aus Fausts Leben* (ten pages in length) constitutes an entity in itself. Müller is interested in showing, in all its emotional intensity, the decisive moment of Faust's confrontation with the devil. A prologue in hell not only serves as a general introduction to the action, but performs the important function of characterizing Mephisto; for the devil, as we shall point out later, is quite different from his prototype in the traditional Faust legend. From the devil we hear of his intense concern for Faust's soul. Twelve years, or half of the contracted time, has elapsed and, according to the agreement, Faust still has one last chance to determine his fate. The second scene has shifted to the court in Madrid, where Faust is completely enamored of the beautiful queen of Aragon. Already he hopes to win her when Mephisto confronts him with a choice between possessing his beloved or returning to his former beggar's existence. With a curse Faust chooses the first alternative and thus loses his soul to hell.

In the *Situation,* the hero shows no depth of character, no desire for noble striving, no inner urge to attain the absolute, but instead is satisfied with achieving sensual fulfillment. As in the puppet play which, incidentally, is Müller's primary source for all his *Faust* creations, Faust is mainly interested in external splendor, material wealth, and the pleasures of life. He reveals his goals to his companion, the skeptical Junker Fritz:

To have delights, which, like nodding young maidens, flit about you and, twitching your ear, lead you from one pleasure to another . . . turn around on your heels, friend, and enjoy completely Gloria mundi![9]

Faust wants to enjoy life and follow his instinctual urges purely for their own sake.

While the Faust figure is taken from literary tradition, Mephisto represents a more independent and personal creation of Müller. Mephisto appears as a devil genius, superior to his consorts in the lower realm, who is only attracted to supermen such as Faust and is, consequently, in a unique position to win his soul. As a devil under the curse of Lucifer's original sin, from which he can never be freed, Mephisto suffers from the burden of his own fate and thus assumes human proportions. In turn, he is a sympathetic evil spirit who shows compassion for Faust and his greatness. But by ascribing to Faust ennobling traits, which seem out of keeping with his previous actions, Mephisto's utterances cause an artistic disunity in the concept of the hero and anticipate his transformation in Müller's sequel, *Fausts Leben*. There is little doubt that in the *Situation* the Mephisto figure is closer to the author's heart than Faust's fate and that the genius of hell admirably reflects Storm and Stress temperament.

Even though the *Situation* is written in explosive, lively language and depicts a highly dramatic episode, it is still a disjointed fragment, unsuitable for the stage. At its publication it received unfavorable reviews.[10] Only Schubart could muster kind words, praising "the fervent imagination of this young genius ... which, almost in danger of singeing its wings, soars in the path of Shakespeare's sun."[11]

Because of the mixed reception which the *Situation* received, Müller let his Faust material rest until Lessing, on a visit to Mannheim in 1777 in behalf of the National theater, provided him with new inspiration. The fragment, *Fausts Leben*, seems to have originated in the second half of 1777 and the beginning of 1778. The drama begins with a prologue, played by the spirits of hell, which discloses marked affinity to the puppet play source. However, whereas the devil scene in the folk drama serves merely to introduce Satan, Müller uses its counterpart as a vehicle of satire directed against the "dull, insipid century."[12] In typical Storm and Stress fashion Lucifer finds contemporary mankind lacking in strength and spirit:

All are enervated from the smallest to the greatest—at the altar and in joyful play ... it's not worth the trouble to play devil among these squashed children of the world, who do not even have enough strength left to sin.[13]

Even the minor devils find man weak and apathetic and blame the age of Rationalism for dulling man's senses and numbing his feeling.

Early in the body of the drama proper Faust recites a long monologue—as is customary for all Faust tales—in which he reveals the poetic conception of his role: he is the titanic, defiant superman who seeks to reach beyond his limits, because he feels dissatisfied in the world in which he is forced to live. Embittered by the realization of his lowly human state and deceitfully robbed of his honor and earthly possessions, he surrenders to the devil. Faust's father comes to warn his son against pursuing a dangerous course, but infernal laughter from the inhabitants of the underworld reminds Faust of his commitment. Resigned to follow through with his plans, he conjures up seven devils of the underworld who act as spokesmen and forerunners of Mephisto. When the latter arrives, Faust sinks into slumber.

Such is the skeletal framework of the action directly involving Faust. The remainder of *Fausts Leben*—roughly two-thirds of the fragment—is filled with episodes which offer in rapid succession, rich, colorful depictions of Jewish moneylenders, boisterous student life, intrigues of Master Knellius, and the cavorting, wenching, and practical joking of the common people. While these scenes portray contemporary life with gusto in true Storm and Stress fashion, they have almost nothing to do either with determining or explaining Faust's character and, hence, must be considered irrelevant to the central theme.

Since *Fausts Leben* is a fragment, it is interesting to conjecture what course the story would have followed if it had been completed. We know from Müller's own statements that the all-important pact scene in the *Situation* was to occur near the end of the second of the five parts projected. It is very likely that the Faust-Mephisto contract, which up to this point is in remarkable agreement with that of the corresponding part of the puppet play, would have been followed throughout. A tragic ending for Faust—at least in the physical sense—would conform to the basically pessimistic philosophy of the age of genius. However, as we shall see, it is possible that Müller planned a kind of moral salvation for his hero.

To return to the fragment as we know it, it is important to determine to what extent Faust is successful in his titanic struggle to throw off the shackles of his lowly existence and to transcend his human limitation. This inner urge to attain the absolute, which is expressed in the preface and again in the long monologue near the beginning of *Fausts Leben*, is still a vital force in one of the final scenes entitled "Fausts Kabinett," where the hero says:

Ha, why does my soul have the insatiable hunger, the unquenchable thirst for ability and accomplishment, knowledge and endeavor, grandeur and honor—the great feeling which raises me, again and again, from the morass of lowliness.[14]

While Faust continually entertains hopes of noble striving, it is ironic that in reality he never realizes his fond dreams; instead, he never rises much higher than his lot in *Situation*, where he is content with achieving sensual fulfillment. Fritz Strich notes correctly that "Müller's *Faust* depicts no ethical or philosophical problem but simply a mundane life."[15] Faust does not penetrate to the inner secrets and mysteries of the universe; rather he seeks out the pleasures of existence. In a conversation with Wagner he lets down his guard when he says "The world could be everything for me."[16] This is in contrast to the viewpoint of Wagner and Faust's father, who, as representatives of Christianity, hope for eternal salvation in another realm.

Metaphysical problems never bother Müller's Faust. As a citizen of Germany in the age of Rationalism, he merely expends his energies in combating those confining bourgeois mores which thwart his genius. His highly charged emotional feelings and his instinctual urge are his guide.

To understand Faust more fully, it is fruitful to study his relations wtih Mephisto and his cohorts in hell. As in the *Situation*, the devils represent different degrees of evil. Just as there are people in this world who rise above the average and aspire to a higher level, so there are among the devils those who are not only slaves of evil, but are imbued with a higher mission and even a moral conscience. To the latter belongs Mephisto. Only *he* is able to comprehend Faust's super nature. Both are exceptional beings and thus have a unique relationship to one another. Mephisto is not only the genius of the underworld, but he is also morally exonerated; for he is blameless, suffering only under the curse of Lucifer's original sin. Love and sympathy attract him to Faust, for, ironically, he is cursed to lead astray the one whom he inwardly loves. This conception of the devil represents a complete break with Christian dogma and prepares the way for a new Faustian concept. For if we equate Mephisto with Faust, as Müller does, at least from the standpoint of their tragic dilemma, then Faust, too, is a condemned person, although he is fundamentally good. That is, from the Rousseauean standpoint he is originally a good man who follows his God-given urges and passions. But spurred on by his instincts to enjoy life to the full and to break the bonds of sterile convention, he links with the devil in his titanic quest. We sympathize with Faust and are willing to grant him moral salvation, for even though his pact is sinful, through it he helps to lead mankind to a fuller realization of life.

But noble as Faust's aspirations are, they do not go beyond the physical life and lack any sign of projecting into the metaphysical realm. In his titanic rantings at the beginning, Faust would search for the absolute, but somehow his hopes are never realized. F. A. Schmidt, in a remarkable doctoral dissertation on Müller's dramatic creations, quite plausibly suggests that Müller's personality did not allow him to project beyond his mundane existence; that in his inability to give his Faust metaphysical depth, Müller vents his frustrations in grotesque formulations. Evidence of the latter would be the grotesque antics of the devils in the eerie twilight of the underworld, the peevish nagging of the Jews (in their dialectal jargon) over financial losses, and the rowdy behavior of the student bullies, such as the senseless beating of their old mentor.[17]

It is in the portrayal of realistic scenes taken from contemporary life that Müller excels. Although these episodes are connected with the Faust theme only in the loosest sense, they are excellent, though overly detailed depictions of the contemporary social milieu. In the tradition of Lenz and Wagner, they offer Müller an excellent chance to satirize weaknesses in contemporary society and culture. We have already mentioned the satirical nature of the prologue, which is directed at social ills in general. Later scenes are aimed at more specific targets. For instance, in the Magister Knellius episode the main character is a caricature of the bookworm type of literary critic. Knellius uses the proper style and slogans, but is actually ignorant, superficial, and boastful. Seuffert believes that the venomous Knellius satire was actually directed at the principal of the Gymnasium in Zweibrücken, G. C. Crollius.[18] In the caricature of the "Gottesspürhund," Müller has selected the well-known apostle of genius, Christof Kaufmann, as his object of ridicule. As a popular figure who rode through the land on his white horse, proclaiming Lavater's doctrine of physiognomy, Müller had met him and was, for a time, entranced by his message, until he realized that the man was nothing but a charlatan.

In addition to individuals, Müller characterizes and satirizes three collective social groups, the first of which are the Jews. Directing mild ridicule at the Jewish moneylender and dealer was common practice in Storm and Stress literature,[19] but no one gave a more vivid picture of this segment of society than Müller. His imitation of the idiom is especially noteworthy. The overly coarse student scene satirizes another element of the population, although, unfortunately, the rich detail contributes much less to the intrinsic unity of the drama than do the student episodes in Lenz's *Hofmeister*. Thirdly, the contemporary law-enforcement officers, represented by the venal and timorous Strick and Fang, are comical, derisible figures like their prototypes in Shakespeare's *Much Ado About Nothing* and Wagner's *Kindsmörderin*.

By presenting, in these scenes of secondary action, accurate pictures of the time, replete with detailed milieu and authentic folk types, Müller has fashioned colorful individual episodes. Unfortunately, these scenes are not linked by any inner purpose or built around a central character, and in their epic and undramatic quality they have value only as isolated contemporary portrayals. Very likely it was Müller's artistic intention to show Faust struggling within the confines of the narrow bourgeois world, propelled, by an inner urge, to throw off the shackles of a stagnant civilization in order to achieve his true potential. In this case, a careful reconstruction of the social milieu would have made sense. But Müller did not succeed in establishing an effective link between Faust and his environs, whereby the deterministic and motivating nature of his surroundings made its presence felt. As it is, Faust, amidst a sea of epic descriptions, is prevented from becoming a strong dramatic figure.

The structure of *Fausts Leben* has also influenced its style and language. The words flow more evenly than, for instance, in the *Situation*, because the epic elements demand a more normal pattern of speech. Since we are primarily interested in the Storm and Stress aspects of style, the episodes forming the secondary action, which are overweighted with descriptive ballast, are of little concern to us. Only where the folk scenes re-create the genuine, coarsely realistic speech of the people do we notice some influence of the program announced by Herder and the young geniuses. Thus the Jews speak pure Palatine dialect, and the members of the lower classes, such as the old shoemaker's wife, express themselves in a colloquial idiom which has a genuine ring.

It is left to Faust and Mephisto, however, in their moments of soul-searching confrontation, to employ a manner of expression which reflects the true Storm and Stress temperament. In the quote below, taken from Faust's soliloquy uttered at the cross-roads in the dark woods at midnight, we feel the Promethean urges, the passionate desires, and the fierce emotional tensions which inspired the young man of genius; here Faust, in his desperation to live life to the full, conjures up the devils of hell, although his conscience advises against it:

Wohlan! steig jetzt in diesen gebannten Zirkel, sicher vor euch und der Hölle—aber wer hemmt meinen Fuss, stockt mir's Blut unterm Herzen?—wie eines Riesen mächtiger Arm liegt's über mir und drängt ab—eine Stimme schmettert durch alle Gebeine: "Tu's nicht!"—Vergebens! ich will, muss—Herauf! herauf! ihr des Unterreichs Geister, herauf, Lichthasser! die ihr auf schwarzen Thronen sitzet, in ewiger Finsternis eure Flüche verheult!—herauf! Faust beschwört euch bei der züchtigenden Sonne—ha![20]

Come on! rise up into this magic circle, safe from yours and from hell. But who holds my foot, stops my heart's blood from flowing? Something like a mighty arm of a giant lies over me and forces me away—a voice resounds through all my limbs: "Don't do it"—to no avail, I want to, I must—come up, come up, you spirits of the underworld, come up, you haters of light, you who sit on black thrones and utter your curses in eternal darkness. Come up! Faust conjures you in the name of the all-ruling sun!

Like a mighty crescendo, the language builds up in intensity, until it peaks in the rite of conjuration. The numerous interjections, inversions, particles, dashes, and repetitions, as well as the short fragmentary sentences and the preponderance of verbs and nouns, all contribute to convey supercharged, chaotic, and illogical feeling.

The passage quoted above, as well as previous references, reveal similarities to Goethe's *Faust;* and it will be fruitful to pursue this relationship. Even though Müller denied seeing Goethe's *Faust* manuscript, he could not help being influenced by Goethean themes and Goethean spirit, which so dominated the young geniuses of the time. If we compare Müller's *Faust* with Goethe's *Urfaust* of 1775, interesting similarities emerge, to which we shall call attention in broad outline. Although the prologue of the devils is missing in Goethe's version, both Faust dramas contain an introductory monologue, scenes of student life, and of a small-town bourgeois milieu. One Faust conjures up an "Erdgeist" and the other a devil. While in Goethe's case the appearance of Mephisto is seemingly motivated, for Müller he becomes Faust's savior from disgrace and misfortune. The Gretchen episode is found in Goethe alone. Both dramas, based, to a great extent, on the puppet play, end with Faust's ruination.

It is in their thought content that the dramas differ most markedly. While both portray a titanic hero seeking to reach out beyond himself, Müller's Faust, in his effort to achieve the absolute, cannot detach himself from this earth. Goethe's hero, on the other hand, aspires to metaphysical goals. And where Müller's Mephisto, his human traits notwithstanding, still reflects the Christian framework of theology, Goethe's "Erdgeist" represents a revolutionary, pantheistic orientation. Esthetically, Goethe's drama, built around a strong central character, attains an inner form which Müller's haphazard episodic arrangement could not achieve, and the dramatic and powerful natural language of Goethe contributes to an uniformity not found in Müller's work. And yet Müller's *Faust* is an independent achievement, inspired by poetic ardor, even though it suffers in comparison with the greater drama.

Because Müller's *Faust* fragment has always been compared to Goethe's work, it has never received much favorable attention and has accordingly exterted little influence. Friedrich Schlegel was the first to acclaim Müller's genius, although he, too, saw many deficiencies in *Faust*.[21] There is some doubt as to whether Müller's drama was ever produced on the stage. Strangely enough, the boisterous student scenes inspired some lesser known dramatists—Soden, Klingemann, Schönemann, Pfizer—in their treatment of the Faust theme. Erich Schmidt first called attention to the fact that Arnim's *Halle und Jerusalem* shows the influence of Müller's *Faust;* Schmidt detects a similar disjointed and episodic form, and the same predilection for painting an overly rich milieu.[22] Both Müller's Faust and Arnim's

Cardenio are titanic supermen, interested in living life to the full.

Before leaving the Faust theme, and for the sake of completeness, we must mention that Müller wrote a third fragment on the same subject, entitled *Fausts Spazierfahrt*. Written in 1777, but not published in book form until 1881,[23] it is a satirical farce, ten pages in length, without any artistic value. Müller's primary purpose was to give Merck and, to a lesser extent, Wieland, a tongue-lashing for writing sharply critical reviews of *Situation aus Fausts Leben*.[24] Even in Rome Müller never let the Faust theme rest and, following Goethe's example, planned a grandiose work on the subject in verse form. Never published, this *Faust* is of no concern to us since the hero was to be no longer a Promethean Storm and Stress type, but a weary, resigned man who placed his trust in eternal salvation.

II Golo und Genoveva

A drama which likewise owes much to Goethe and bears unmistakable Storm and Stress characteristics is *Golo und Genoveva*. Although it was written between 1775 and 1781, it was not published until 1811, when Tieck interceded on Müller's behalf. Without doubt, *Golo und Genoveva* is the most pleasing and most mature of Müller's dramatic creations, and along with the idylls belongs to the best that the poet has written. A critic writing in 1936[25] still endorsed Hettner's statement that next to *Götz* it is the most significant drama of the Storm and Stress period;[26] today, however, we would substitute Lenz's *Soldaten* or even *Der Hofmeister*.

With *Götz*, Müller's play shares the same irrelevancies of plot, the same multiplicity of scenes, and the same German medieval setting. Based on the "Volksbuch" and the puppet play of the same name, *Golo und Genoveva* owes much of its subject matter to its historical and legendary sources, but the poetic aura which suffuses it is the author's own creation. The basic framework of the story is the traditional one: when the Palatine Count Siegfried leaves home to fight the Moors in the middle of the eighth century, he designates the knight Golo to be in charge while he is gone. Golo falls in love with Siegfried's wife, Genoveva, and the remainder of the drama is a record of his soul in travail. Should he follow his conscience and renounce his love, or should he follow his instinctual urges and court Genoveva? Golo's benefactress, the evil Mathilde (who later turns out to be his mother), persuades him to pursue the latter course, which leads to his downfall. Müller's version provides a conciliatory ending, at least as far as Genoveva is concerned.

Although the story is laid in a specific historical period, this is not a historical drama in the sense that *Götz* is. Müller merely uses the legend as a starting point and makes no effort to reconstruct the cultural atmosphere of the time or to clothe his characters and scenes with the trappings of the period. The drama teems with anachronisms, but this is no concern of the author, for instead of giving us a historical perspective, he is more interested in painting the natural landscape which is native both to the story and Müller's home. In turn, this landscape reflects and influences the moods of the characters, whose psychological complexity forms the real essence of the drama. In Friedrich Gundolf's words, "Müller's characters receive their life from the milieu in which they move. Therefore his real art form is the idyll ... even his longer creations are merely idyllic episodes and not dramas."[27] Although this statement is not pertinent to *Faust*, it is valid for *Golo und Genoveva*. This latter drama is, without a doubt, Müller's most subjective work, mirroring the most personal and heartfelt impressions of his early life before Mannheim. Showing the influence of Herder and Goethe, Maler Müller during his Storm and Stress period was of the firm conviction that a work of art must reflect man's genuine experiences and that it must represent the organic and vital element of existence.

We can rightly speak of a Werther mood in *Golo und Genoveva*. In Goethe's and Müller's creations, nature molds man, and in a reverse sense man demonstrates his power by choosing to observe only certain aspects of nature which, in turn, will influence him. Thus nature and man form a unity in which the divine operates and reveals itself. The rolling hills of the Palatinate, with its wooded peaks, its fertile vineyards, and the summer countryside redolent of growing grass and moldering forest soil, seem to be reflected in the native people that emerge in the drama. Types such as the gardener Adam, his wife Margrethe, Adolf, and Steffens have their roots in the Palatine hills and vales.

Above all, nature sets the mood for the emotional state of the characters; the physical surroundings, in their varying aspects, correspond to the many-sided and changing human dispositions. Müller shows here, as well as in *Faust*, his predilection for the somber atmosphere of night. A warm, sultry summer night is the time when Mathilde reveals her vile plan (II, 4); in an identical atmosphere, Golo commits his crime, for only in the darkness can he pass for Dragones (III, 4). There are innumerable instances where midnight is accompanied by unrest and expectation, and it is at this hour that Golo experiences tormenting pangs of conscience (IV, 16), reminding us of similar scenes in Klinger's *Zwillinge*. The seasons, too, reflect human moods. It has been pointed out that "Spring holds sway over the chaste love of Golo, high summer over the passionate, lustful outbreaks, and melancholy fall over the gloomy consequences, regret, and death."[28] The above cases in point give ample evidence that Müller—landscape painter as well as poet—devotes much of the drama's economy to the description of nature. Colorful as this description is, it is obvious that, because of it, the rigid construction that drama demands must suffer.

To a certain extent, Müller's descriptive and undramatic approach is justified. If we begin with the premise that Müller, like Klinger and Leisewitz, regarded the true dramatic action as taking place, not externally, but in the soul of the hero, and if we further stipulate that the finite environment fulfills a symbolic function, it follows that an expansive, moodlike description of nature would fit Müller's intent better than a preponderance of robust, external action. We believe that the heart of the drama, the element which gives it unity, is the depiction of Golo's soul in travail. Already Müller's *Faust* revealed an inner vacillation, an inherent weakness, and a lack of steadfastness. But his tragic and emotional conflict is caused by his inability to attain the titanic, superhuman nature for which he strives so earnestly. In the character of Faust, Müller may be said to have given poetic expression to his own apparent difficulty in realizing his Storm and Stress aspirations. Golo's uncertainties, on the other hand, are of a purely human nature and stem from a passionate love for a woman whom he can not and may not attain. The vital actuality of Golo's frustration bespeaks an intensely personal note and most likely reflects Müller's emotional crisis during the days of his courtship of Charlotte Kärner.

An important deviation of Müller's drama from the legendary source—the purity of Golo's love, unstained by sensual desire— as it is manifest in the first two acts, seems to be occasioned by personal experience. Soliloquizing in the first act about his love for Genoveva, Golo says: "Could you ever go astray... No!—My heart is completely pure. Do I love her? And even if I do, my heart is pure. This I swear before God."[29] Golo's love is pure because it stems from his innermost soul, and his passion is not sinful because it is given to him by God. That is, according to the Storm and Stress conception, man's ethos is based on his instinctual urges, and consequently Golo experiences no emotional conflict.

Since Golo cannot be bad, the story needs an antagonist to embody evil, and this is where Mathilde fits in. She not only stimulates the action, but makes Golo conscious of his dark urges and then effectively promotes them. As his benefactress Mathilde fans his passionate desires and masterminds his unsuccessful attempt to abduct Genoveva from the castle (III, 4). From this point on, two souls struggle in Golo's breast —one moment, mindful of his friendship for Siegfried, he would renounce his loved one, and the next he is filled with a lustful passion to possess her. But through the overpowering influence of Mathilde, who calls herself a "Deus ex machina,"[30] his wicked nature wins out and the gentle knight turns into a demonic, ruthless madman. The conflict within him between heartlessness and repentant realization of his evil course rages anew (IV, 7) until, once again, evil asserts itself when Golo murders the noble knight, Karl. Golo blames the innocent Genoveva for his misdeed: "The murderess! She forced me to murder... I wish she lay buried under the ground."[31]

Only when Golo believes that accomplices of Mathilde have murdered Genoveva does he come to his senses and realize the source of all evil. He thrusts his sword into Mathilde's side; and although she survives, her days are short-lived. For Golo, too, there is no hope. Shocked by the sight of Genoveva alive and well, he collapses under the heavy burden of guilt and asks for forgiveness: "Pardon me, before I die."[32] His wish is granted.

It is through the depiction of the figure of Golo that the drama becomes a work of art. Maler Müller uses his best talents to lay bare the soul of a man tormented by love and hate, for in Golo's existential state he expresses his own feelings and emotions. When, after an expression of the criminal intent, pangs of conscience drive Golo to madness, the poet is re-creating his own experiences. When Müller forsook his beloved and her child, he was just as guilty as Golo, and in the drama's conciliatory ending he seeks refuge from personal condemnation.

A common motif—the impossibility of possessing one's beloved—links Golo with Werther. But whereas Genoveva could have provided Golo with the fulfillment of all his dreams, Lotte could not have alleviated Werther's deepest afflictions. *Werther* has cosmic and metaphysical implications which are completely lacking in Müller's work. As already mentioned, *Werther* and *Golo und Genoveva* are closely akin in their depiction of nature. In both, nature and nature moods influence and sustain the action, for both heroes do not act but react, either to an inner feeling or to an external motivation. In stories such as these, where action and mood coincide, the true action takes place within the soul of the hero.

The most forceful person in the drama, the one who propels the plot and the dramatic action, is Mathilde. A colorful representative of the "Machtweib" figure so popular in German literature at this time, she is a demonically enchanting woman full of unbridled energy, who ruthlessly carries out her evil deeds. She expresses her basic philosophy to Golo as follows: "To suffer and to allow myself to be overwhelmed was never my nature; rather, I preferred to inflict my will on others, to hold the whip high and lash soundly ... until I attain, what I want."[33] Sensual and beautiful, she holds everybody under her spell. She enjoys a relationship with the Bishop of Trier, as Goethe's Adelheid does with the Bishop of Bamberg; she gains the confidence of Dragones and uses him to carry out her intrigues, just as Adelheid does with Franz.

It is quite obvious that Adelheid in *Götz* is a model for Mathilde. Mathilde controls Golo's actions in the manner in which Adelheid determines Weislingen's course. Both women are enterprising and ambitious: Adelheid wants to control a

monarchy and Mathilde a dukedom. Both upbraid their pro-
tégés, Golo and Weislingen, for being depressed and indecisive,
although in neither case do they forsake the knights in their
melancholy moods. Müller, however, often intensifies the characteristics of Adelheid in his Mathilde and has her speak a
coarse coachman's language when she wants to give vent to
her fury and indignation. A modern Lulu who mesmerizes the
sundry males who cross her path, she is exonerated, to some
extent, by her sincere love for her son.

The lovable personage of Genoveva appears as a contrast
to Mathilde. Although she is not the pious, saintly person of
the legend, she personifies ideal human qualities. An aura of
gentility and purity surrounds her at all times, and in her
infinite capacity for sacrificial love and forgiveness Müller
may be paying tribute again to the loved one of his Zweibrücken days. Genoveva's two most prized possessions, her
honor and her child, sustain her during her tribulation. Her
son Schmerzenreich—as is typical of children in Storm and
Stress dramas—is a paragon of innocence and naïveté, a mani-
festation of pure nature.

The countless other figures whose adventures and fates form
the secondary action of the drama are only of passing interest
to us. Doubtlessly Müller envisioned this rich episodic depiction as a backdrop, to illumine the better the motivations and
feelings of Golo and, to a lesser extent, of Genoveva. But as in
Faust, the link between the actions of the heroes and those of
the minor characters is a weak one. And in Müller's all-con-
suming effort to lay bare the inner experiences of Golo in their
most sensitive and emotional nuances, he neglects subplots by
never carrying them to completion. A case in point concerns
a minor love affair between Golo and Anne, Genoveva's lady-
in-waiting. Although Anne is secretly enamored of Golo, we
hear no more of her love when she returns to the court after
a long absence; and Golo is never aware of her feeling for him.
As noted earlier several characters deserve praise, if only because they are genuine representations of the Palatine folk.
And following in the tradition of Storm and Stress drama, Müller
has the lower segment of society speak in pure dialect. In this
particular play, it is the two murderers hired to kill Genoveva
who speak the true Palatine idiom which Müller learned as a

child. By way of illustration, we quote a conversation between the first and second murderer, as they gather up their courage and make final preparations to kill the noble woman:

ZWEITER MÖRDER: Gieb's her, noch'n Schluck. Na, fang weil an.
ERSTER MÖRDER: Brur, frog mol, ob se schun gebetet.
ZWEITER MÖRDER: Vor was? Hon's sunst als nie thon, wann mer umbrocht.
ERSTER MÖRDER: Is e ander Korn, morde jetzt gerichtlich.[34]

SECOND MURDERER: Give it to me. One more gulp. Well, let's start.
FIRST MURDERER: Brother, ask her whether she has prayed yet.
SECOND MURDERER: Why? We never did it other times when we killed someone.
FIRST MURDERER: She's of a different mold, we'll murder properly.

Despite the disjointed and episodic arrangement of the scenes, a fine lyrical mood which pervades throughout gives the play a certain poetic unity and charm. More than twenty lyrical passages in verse form, one of which is three pages in length, are interspersed in the dialogue and give *Golo und Genoveva* the semblance of an opera or musical drama. The dirge, "Mein Grab sei unter Weiden," which Golo sings again and again during the course of the drama, serves as a kind of leitmotif and mirrors his character. The inclusion of such an abundance of lyrics represents a Romantic element and influenced the form of the dramas of Tieck, Arnim, and Brentano.

That Müller threw the Aristotelian dramatic unities to the wind is obvious from the foregoing discussion. There are more changes of scene than in *Götz*—in Pfalzl castle alone the action takes place in sixteen different rooms. An interval of four years separates the fourth act from the fifth, which is an indication of the epic nature of the happenings. We have previously mentioned how the main action of the drama tends to be lost in a maze of secondary plots involving a host of characters. Müller's philosophy for fashioning an inner structure for his drama seems to be best expressed by one of his characters, the architect Erwin. When asked about his plans for building the Strassburg cathedral, he says: "Not according to practice and rule; but following my heart, as God showed me."[35] Incidentally, the injection of Erwin von Steinbach into the drama is an anachronism, for the master-builder of Gothic cathedrals, immortalized in Goethe's *Von deutscher Baukunst,* lived five hundred years after the Moorish wars.

With the exception of the lyrical elements, the language of the drama has a realistic tone about it, with the common people especially using the peculiar idiom, colloquialisms, and proverbs of the Palatinate in their speech. In general, the style is more even than in *Faust,* and the instances of Storm and Stress language are few. On the other hand, there are a number of idyllic scenes, with the forest scenes (Genoveva and Schmerzenreich) conveying a special sense of inner truth. Likewise, those episodes in which nature determines the mood are written in an inspired tone, testifying to the painter-poet's predilection for creating scenes in which man and nature blend. Although *Golo und Genoveva* does not have a dramatic style in the strict sense of the word, in its artistic expression it represents a step forward when compared to *Faust.*

Golo und Genoveva must be judged solely as a closet drama, for it never enjoyed a stage performance in Müller's lifetime or in succeeding generations. The play had its premiere in Mannheim in 1924, but met with no success.[36] Understandably, its influence on subsequent plays on the same theme was limited. It came into Tieck's hands, in manuscript form, in 1797, and undoubtedly suggested the story for his *Leben und Tod der heiligen Genoveva* (1799). Müller even accused Tieck of plagiarism. But Tieck's *Genoveva* is a typically Romantic work; the scenes show little action, and a Romantic haze envelops them. Besides, Tieck emphasizes the saintly and religious qualities of his Genoveva rather than the purely human ones. Raupach, Hebbel, and Otto Ludwig wrote plays on the same theme, and although they must have known Müller's work, they did not incorporate much of its spirit.

Another work by Müller written in 1778, *Niobe,* is only of passing interest to us, since it is actually an opera. Although its story is classical, it incorporates the mood of Goethe's *Prometheus,* exhibiting provocative defiance and inflammatory desire for vengeance. Niobe is a superhuman figure who seeks to overstep the bounds of life and be the equal of the gods. Like *Faust, Niobe* stresses the superiority of the truly vital person over the Christian God, who is chastised for negating life. However, Müller is no more successful than he was in *Faust* in giving his titanic figures inner life. Since he himself lacked the ability to transcend his pedestrian existence and project himself into the infinite, he was unable to endow his super-heroine with flesh and blood. Thus Niobe remains a phantom. In style *Niobe* is a transitional work in which Müller abandons the crass, exaggerated style of genius for a more subdued and measured speech. This drama points the way to the Classical plays of the Roman period and clearly belongs to another literary movement.

It is the two Storm and Stress plays, *Faust* and *Golo und Genoveva*, though, which establish Maler Müller as a dramatist. Even if they show a lack of inner concentration and of formative power, they contain a subjective element which gives them a poetic and emotional vitality; they mirror the author's own inner discord and his anguished search for clarity.

CHAPTER 5

Friedrich Maximilian Klinger:
Youthful Exuberance in the Spirit of Genius

THE dramatist Klinger is often regarded as both the most forceful and the most radical exponent of the Storm and Stress spirit.
In the center of his dramas stands the "Kraftkerl," the hero possessing a surplus of energy and passion, for which he must find
an outlet. The hero is primarily concerned with existential problems of a purely personal nature; he feels compelled to express
his disgust with a malevolent universe by means of fervent moral
convictions and unbridled passions. Unleashing the instinctive,
ethereal emotions of man seems to be a goal, for through this
irrational element the new man overcomes his frustrations and
experiences his true self intoxicatingly in its greatest intensity and
fullness. Berendt calls the "raging, stamping, snorting, climbing,
eerie-staring, twitching, roaring, howling...the essential and
primary element" in Klinger's Storm and Stress dramas.[1]

Unlike Lenz and Wagner, Klinger was not interested in depicting in detail the realistic social milieu of the contemporary
world with its attendant problems; nor was he concerned with
painting quiet, idyllic landscape moods in the manner of Maler
Müller. Likewise, the metaphysical problems of the heroes of
Goethe's youthful works were not transferred to the dramas of
his disciple. Rather, Klinger's art is quite independent of the external world and time, the pure expression of an animated soul.
The exceptional people who populate his Storm and Stress
dramas do not represent the lower-class milieu but are for the
most part members of the court in an exotic legendary or historical locale. In this atmosphere, Klinger does not have to reproduce faithfully the spirit of an age; instead he creates tempestuous scenes in which his heroes can let off steam by addressing
rhetorical and extravagant tirades to the universe. Although
Klinger's art has a different emphasis than that of the dramatists
we have previously discussed, it nevertheless has many elements

in common with the works already treated and can best be understood within the framework of the Storm and Stress movement.

Friedrich Maximilian Klinger was born at a focal center of young genius, Frankfurt. The year of his birth, 1752, is the same as Leisewitz', a year after Lenz's, three after Goethe's and Maler Müller's, and five after Wagner's. Klinger's family was of limited means. The father died while Klinger was still a child, and the family financial situation became even more precarious. The mother earned money as a washerwoman, and young Friedrich did private tutoring and performed other, more menial tasks to help defray his expenses at the "Gymnasium." During these pre-university years, he made Goethe's acquaintance and met every Saturday with the young geniuses in a restaurant in the Rittergasse. Goethe describes him as being "tall, slender, and well-built with regular features." He also mentions that Klinger's "demeanor was neither friendly nor repulsive, and, if the man was not seething inside, it was restrained." Goethe was especially impressed by his self-reliance and firmness of character,[2] which was quite in contrast to the image he had formed of Lenz.

In 1774, with financial assistance from Goethe, Klinger went to the University of Giessen to study law. But, encouraged by his patron, he spent more time in playwriting than in strictly academic pursuits. By the time he broke off his studies in May, 1776, he had already completed *Otto* (1775), *Das leidende Weib* (1775), *Die Zwillinge* (1776), and *Simsone Grisaldo* (1776), and had done preliminary sketches of other Sturm und Drang dramas. Needless to say, Klinger was a most prolific writer in these years when he enjoyed Goethe's companionship and the stimulating, interacting influence of Wagner, Lenz, and Müller. Lavater, Basedow, Claudius, Klopstock, Schubart, Heinse, Jacobi, and the Stolberg brothers were also on familiar terms with Klinger and helped develop his creative talents.

As for literary influences, along with Goethe's *Götz* and *Werther*, it was Rousseau's writings which made a profound impression on him. Already in his school years in Frankfurt he read *Emile* in the original, and throughout his life Rousseau remained his guiding star. Rousseauean spirit provides the unifying link between his Storm and Stress dramas and his later literary works, even though a wide gap separates them in content and emphasis. Like Emile, Klinger considered himself a child of nature who had to rise from humble beginnings; but Klinger felt no need to follow the Rousseauean dictum and shed his overcivilized, over-refined cloak, because he never possessed it. Thus he considered himself one of the purest disciples of the gospel of nature. Besides his natural affinity for Rousseau, Klinger shared with his Storm and Stress compatriots a deep veneration for Shakespeare, whom he knew in the Wieland translation. As we shall see in the analyses of the individual dramas, the spirit, form, and content of the Shakespearean plays left their imprint on his works.

In typical Rousseauean fashion, Klinger writes to Boie on January 13, 1776: "I hate everything about academic life."[3] After he had left the university abruptly, Klinger lived in various towns searching for a career and for his place in life. Because of his creative efforts in the field of drama he considered a career in the theater, and his natural penchant for heroic adventure led him to consider joining up with military forces in the cause of the American Revolution. Frequently he returned to his native city, and, as mentioned previously, it was in Frankfurt that Klinger and Schleiermarcher welcomed Lenz so ceremoniously, when the latter stopped off in the spring of 1776 en route to Weimar.

Klinger, too, followed his idol Goethe to Weimar, where he remained from June through September, 1776, and where he became acquainted with life at a court for the first time. In the beginning, his letters are filled with a feeling of ecstatic happiness and hope: "On Monday I arrived.—Lay on Goethe's breast, and he embraced me fervently and affectionately.... Wherever I look there is balsam for my heart and spirit."[4] But soon his frustrations haunted him once more, for he says: "I am without goal and purpose, as I was originally, and let everything take its course."[5] And in the same vein: "I move about in continual confusion and flee hither and thither from myself, the most terrible one."[6] It was in this state of mind that he wrote the drama *Sturm und Drang*, which originally bore the title "Der Wirrwarr" (confusion). Klinger's restless and exuberant nature gradually began to bother Goethe, who writes in a letter to Lavater of September 16, "Klinger is a splinter in our flesh."[7] Goethe's cooling attitude toward him hurt Klinger to the quick, and it was twenty years before cordial relations between the two men were resumed.

After leaving Weimar, Klinger took a post as theater-poet in the Seyler troupe of actors, the same organization with which Wagner was associated. From October, 1776, until February, 1778, he accompanied the company from Leipzig to Dresden, Gotha, Mannheim, Cologne, Frankfurt, and Mainz. Influenced by his itinerant existence, he adopted Bohemian habits, contracted debt, and fell into a prolonged state of depression. A quote from a letter to Schleiermacher—"I must go away! away!"[8]—illustrates his resolve to turn over a new leaf.

At this juncture in his life, Klinger's Storm and Stress period ends rather abruptly, and with it his favored position as a leading contemporary dramatist. Only the political tragedy *Stilpo und seine Kinder*, written in 1777 but not published until 1780, represents a significant addition to the dramatic creations of the age of genius. His later plays, written in a different vein, rarely appeared on the German stage.

Goethe's brother-in-law, Schlosser, who had sought to rehabilitate Lenz, also came to Klinger's rescue and was instrumental in securing for the latter a lieutenant's rank in a volunteer corps raised by the Austrians for the War of the Bavarian Succession. The war ended after a year, but in this time Klinger realized that he had found his calling and was bent on spending the rest of his life in military service. To Kayser he wrote in 1779: "My vocation is and will remain that of a soldier. . . . Where the war is, there am I."[9] Through the efforts of influential patrons in Württemberg, Klinger in 1780 obtained a commission in a Russian battalion of marines. Spending the rest of his days in Russia, he rose rapidly in his career: he was a commandant of an important cadet school, an influential adviser at the court, and a distinguished army officer. At his death in 1831 he was curator of the University of Dorpat and a lieutenant-general in the Russian army.

Klinger remained unusually productive in Russia, with the new responsibilities occasioned by his governmental and military positions giving him a balance of character which tempered the tone of his novels and dramas. His best dramas approach the tolerant, human spirit of Goethe's *Iphigenie*, and the novels are a composite of Rationalism and Classicism, reminiscent of the older Wieland. All that is left of his Storm and Stress was a Rousseauean yearning for the simple life and the criticism of the decadent courts. Since we are primarily concerned with

Klinger's dramas of the age of genius, we shall omit discussion of the later literary works and return to the plays written in the spirit of youthful exuberance.

Klinger's first work, the knightly drama *Otto* (1775), borrows heavily from *Götz von Berlichingen* and Shakespeare's *King Lear*. Like the author's later dramas it employs a fictitious story and a vague historical setting without local color, but it shares with *Götz* the theme of the dissolution of the knightly order, similar dramatic figures, and even similar scenes and dialogues. Scenes of gigantic proportions, similar to those in *King Lear*, also appear and reflect the Shakespearean spirit as interpreted by the "Stürmer und Dränger." Otto suffers emotional crises, in which he is overcome by his passions (in the manner of King Lear), but crass exaggerations in language and characterization show that Klinger has not yet mastered his art. Of passing interest is the fact that this early drama employs a favorite Storm and Stress motif, that of the unequal and dissimilar brothers who are at odds with their father.

Showing his continuing dependence on dramatic models, Klinger used as a prototype for his second play, *Das leidende Weib* (1775), namely Lenz's drama of social involvement, *Der Hofmeister*. He even copied the names of characters from Lenz, for a "Läuffer" and a "Geheimderat" are numbered among the dramatis personae. Employing the loose, episodic structure of *Der Hofmeister*, Klinger's drama has thirty-three scenes which depict realistically but somewhat forcedly an eighteenth-century social milieu. The conflict between burgher and decadent aristocracy does not have Lenzian overtones of cynical despair about it, but ends on a Rousseauean note; the survivors of a tumultuous, grief-shrouded life seek their peace in a rural countryside amidst farms and orchards.

As in Lenz's model, the court aristocracy is treacherous, corrupt, ruthless, and immoral, and the author's sympathies lie with the victimized lower middle class. The upper class is not always defiled by the mores of their society, but by evil external influences: the envoy's wife commits adultery, we are led to believe, because she was led astray by Wieland's novels. A series of erotic love affairs which bridge the different strata of society serve to muddle and intensify social conflicts; however, after the third act Klinger gradually loses interest in maladies of a communal nature and, instead, shifts his focus to the psychological problems of the individual caught in the web of an unhappy love affair. It is in depicting a tormented soul that Klinger has found his element. Concerned more in expressing feeling than in giving it relevance, he uses violent, passionate language replete with interjections, half-sentences, inarticulate exclamations, and illogical utterings, to express great emotion. In this experimental drama, Klinger came to realize that the episodic and realistic play on a contemporary social theme, as Lenz had developed it, was not his forte; rather, he was to select henceforth a more unified plot built around a powerful, exceptional, and even improbable individual, who could roar out at the injustices of the universe. Instead of using the terse, reserved, and distraught speech of Lenz's characters, Klinger's heroes were to express themselves, from here on, in a booming, bombastic language, reminiscent of the Baroque period.

I   Die Zwillinge

Klinger's next work, *Die Zwillinge* (1776), is his first completely independent and, at the same time, most significant drama artistically. When, in 1775, the impresario Schröder of Hamburg offered a prize for the best new tragedy, three works were submitted: a drama about two unlucky brothers by an anonymous author, *Julius von Tarent* by Leisewitz, and *Die Zwillinge*. All three, strangely enough, had plots built around the theme of fratricide, and it is possible that through his good friend, J. M. Miller, who was in close touch with the poets of the Göttingen "Hainbund," Klinger heard of the intentions of Leisewitz to compete. He may even have known some details about *Julius von Tarent*, so that the resemblance of theme may have been more than coincidence. But Klinger's play is nevertheless original; its style and method are the author's own. *Die Zwillinge* won the prize, mainly because the fierce, elemental passion generated by the main hero caught most accurately the spirit of the time. *Julius von Tarent*, which will be discussed in the next chapter, is a much more careful and deliberate piece of stagecraft in the Lessing tradition, but it lacks the inner fire of Klinger's drama.

According to the stipulations a drama, to be eligible for

Schröder's prize, had to fulfill certain general conditions: it should be stageworthy, require no expensive costumes nor excessive use of stage props, and the number of characters were to be kept to a reasonable minimum.[10] Very likely because of these external demands Klinger used a rigid dramatic structure in the Classical sense. In direct contrast to the disjointed, episodic arrangement of *Otto* and *Das leidende Weib*, the action of *Die Zwillinge* is of a very unified nature. The number of characters is restricted to seven, and the scene never moves from the castle of Guelfo's father. Instead of using the locale of his contemporary homeland, Klinger has transferred the scene to the Italian Renaissance, without intending, however, to supply any historical or cultural atmosphere. The play, beginning in the afternoon and continuing until the next morning, stays well within a twenty-four-hour limit. Because of the taut and compact construction, Klinger was able to achieve an effect of great intensity in keeping with the main theme.

The plot is of the simplest: Guelfo, about whom the whole story revolves, is a twin who is obsessed by the nagging suspicion that he is not the second-born, as his parents and superiors have asserted, but was born first and, consequently, has been cheated out of the privileges and powers which accrue to the first son. His brother, Ferdinando, will inherit the ducal crown, his material possessions, and even win the girl Guelfo loves—all because fate has been unkind to him. Guelfo's frustrations and feelings of injustice gradually deteriorate into madness, and in his dire emotional straits he kills his twin brother, when the latter refuses to renounce his rights as the would-be heir. In order to shield the family from further disgrace, the father stabs Guelfo to death.

In this play, in which the action is kept to the barest minimum, the stabbing of Guelfo is the most significant occurrence that transpires on the stage. Other important events take place behind the scenes. Guelfo's quarrel with his father takes place between the second and third acts, and the fratricide between the third and fourth. The arrival of the bridal couple (II, 1) and the report of the riderless horse are narrated dramatically; but again these are events the spectators never see. Significantly, the first three acts begin with a conversation between Guelfo and his foil, Grimaldi, for Guelfo clearly dominates the story. Actually, in the twenty-one scenes of the play he is absent in only seven (II, 2–4; IV, 1–3; V, 1), and his emotional development determines the course of the action.

In Guelfo, Klinger has created an ideal untamed and powerful Storm and Stress type, who is angry with the universe and expresses his frustrations in passionate outbursts. Guelfo's emotions reach such an intoxicating intensity that we get the impression that he not only is ranting against the grave injustices that have befallen him, but that he actually takes a rapturous delight in the agitated feelings themselves which external conditions have induced. Shaken to the very quick by circumstances of his unjust fate, Guelfo, in his emotional fervor, sets free his inner nature and experiences life to the full. That Guelfo's temperament reflects Klinger's own is born out by a confession which the dramatist made in a letter to Schumann, dated February, 1775. Like the hero of *Die Zwillinge*, Klinger feels that his honor has been hurt, and his pathos reaches great heights as he writes:

Passions, unknown to me, tear me apart. . . . They would be the undoing of anyone else. . . . Every moment I would like to hurl the human race and everything that teems and stirs into chaos to be devoured, and plunge after it myself. But enough of that, I know this feeling will pass and then I will laugh. . . . I have to laugh about this letter . . . to entertain such gripes in my heart.[11]

From the latter part of the quotation it is obvious that Klinger generated passions for their own sake, and that letting off steam in this manner had a therapeutic effect on him.

The first scene sets the pattern for the play. We are introduced to an enraged Guelfo, "with a staring glance that gnaws from within,"[12] who hates his brother with a passion that can scarcely be contained any longer. Alternately his tensions are increased and then relaxed through conversations and by means of various types of sensory stimuli. When Grimaldi reminds him of how the Duke bestowed favors on Ferdinando and helped the latter to win the beautiful Countess Kamilla, Guelfo bristles with envy; and when Grimaldi recalls his friend's brave deeds of the past, this heightens Guelfo's sense of injustice. Drinking wine and listening to Grimaldi play soft tunes on the piano soothes him, but stronger, darker notes and heavier wine have an opposite effect. At the end of the scene Guelfo emerges as an angry young man who "beats his forehead with his fist and howls with the winds."[13]

The ebb-and-flow technique of manipulating the emotions continues throughout the drama, although Guelfo's feelings are always aroused more than they are placated, until they bring about
the catastrophic situation in which Guelfo kills his brother.

Since the method outlined above remains the same for the remaining acts and scenes, we will call attention only to those cli-
mactic scenes in which Guelfo's emotional tensions are increased
alarmingly. Doctor Galbo's vague answer to Guelfo's question as
to who actually was born first transports the hero into a mad
frenzy (I, 2), and Grimaldi knows how to prolong this state of
mind. Next his father irritates Guelfo by contrasting Ferdinando's
intelligence with his own hotheadedness (I, 4). When his mother
promises Guelfo a gift for his future bride, this effort at appease-
ment works in reverse, for he is reminded of the beautiful dap-
ple-gray horse which was given as a dowry to the favored
Ferdinando.

In the second act, Guelfo is badly upset when he looks out of
the window and sees the bridal pair, Ferdinando and Kamilla,
arrive. Envisioning Ferdinando's future happiness, which should
rightfully be his lot, he entertains the first thought of revenge.
When Guelfo has a private conversation with Kamilla a little
later, he realizes that he has lost her forever and is driven to dis-
traction (II, 5). Curses, threatening speeches, sobbing, and la-
menting reveal his state of mind. The climax of the drama occurs
at the opening of the third act and in the gloom of night. Earlier
in the evening and off stage, the father has literally kicked Guelfo
out of the house for acting like a mad dog. Also between scenes
Guelfo gets hold of a contract which bequeathes all of the family's possessions to Ferdinando. In anger and desperation he wanders about in the dark and plans revenge on the brother. His
words "Grimaldi! I must! I must!"[14] represent the dramatic climax.

As if beset by a demon, Guelfo concentrates all his energies
and passions on the pursuit of one goal, that of eradicating his
brother. This catastrophic event takes place off stage between the
third and fourth acts. Confronting his brother in the forest,
Guelfo demands of him either the satisfaction of being the firstborn or of obtaining Kamilla's hand. When Ferdinando refuses
to grant him either alternative, he presses toward him, and as
Ferdinando cries "Kamilla," Guelfo can no longer contain his
passions, kills his brother, and laughs scornfully into the forest

(IV, 5). In a crazed state, he breaks out in infernal laughter and, because he can no longer face himself, breaks the mirror (IV, 4). After a short sleep, he is resigned to meet his doom.

In this drama of baroque contrasts, the tempestuous outbursts alternate with peaceful moments, which serve to give Guelfo a brief respite from his inner tensions and which, when they occur, accentuate all the more the passionate tirades. We have already mentioned the palliative effect which wine and music exert on Guelfo. Later on, thoughts of an escapist nature soothe him; he envisions riding on a donkey to the Turks (I, 5), or cooling off his emotions in war (II, 2), or soaring on a sunbeam above the cares of the world (II, 5). Grimaldi suggests that he renounce the world and become a hermit (II, 1). At another time Guelfo finds release by taking his pistol and shooting into the air (II, 1), and his father recalls how he pacifies his wild nature by going to the forest and bathing his hands in the blood of wild animals (II, 2). From the beginning of the third act until the end of the drama, Guelfo increasingly seeks solace in sleep, which symbolically anticipates his final salvation in death.

The ebb and flow of emotional conflict within Guelfo's breast is influenced not only by impersonal external factors, but by individuals as well. Thus the principal male characters—Grimaldi, Ferdinando, and father Guelfo—serve to stimulate Guelfo's violent passions, while the two female figures—Kamilla and Amalia —act as healing balm for Guelfo's feverish nature. With reference to Grimaldi father Guelfo says: "He is a gloomy man, who runs about at night in the fields, in storm and wind, and calls to the stars. The cemetery is said to be his favorite abode."[15] With his Ossianic night thoughts and melancholy delight in death, Grimaldi represents the eternal pessimist who is sick both physically and spiritually and has lost the strength and willpower to assert himself. His personality has an opposite effect on Guelfo. The latter rebels against Grimaldi's weaknesses by becoming the savage and ruthless man of action and by hurling wild tirades at the universe. Grimaldi, the apostle of Weltschmerz, even assumes the role of an intriguer, who incites envy of the "sweet, sensitive, intelligent Ferdinando"[16] in the hero by recalling to mind Guelfo's former exploits. It is Grimaldi, more than anyone else, who fans Guelfo's emotions to the point where he must take revenge.

Because of the very theme of the drama, the twin brother Ferdinando assumes a central role, for he is the salient target of Guelfo's wrath and frustration. The theme of fratricide, which dates back to the Cain and Abel story in the Bible and to the Classical legend of Atreus and Thyestes, appealed particularly to the age of genius. No subject was better suited to portray the blind force of human passion, which even severed blood ties and destroyed a family in its wake. Although alleged family favoritism plays a part, it is above all the contrast in temperaments of the brothers which causes the sharp conflict. Father Guelfo detects the difference in his sons, describing Ferdinando as "the one who gains more through intelligence, because he is quieter, more deliberate, and takes advantage of an opportunity."[17] On the other hand, he reproaches his second son for not "directing his wild spirit into good channels, and not allowing his valor to be guided by Ferdinando's intelligence."[18] Ferdinando embodies the well-mannered, worldly-wise, prudent young noble who has been educated to perpetuate the ideals of the Rococo age. Revolting against the strict rules of conduct of a degenerate court society, Guelfo, as a true "Stürmer and Dränger," relies on his instinctual urges and unbridled passions to guide him. He becomes so incensed at the misdirected society represented by his brother that he has to indulge in excesses; the misdeeds and brutalities he commits are evidences of his frustrations.

The father's natural antipathy to Guelfo likewise serves to increase the tension in Guelfo's breast. Instead of their being contrasted to each other, the son is actually a duplication of the father. After all, the hero's father is always referred to as "der alte Guelfo" and shares with his offspring the same passionate, proud nature.

While the father incites Guelfo's emotions, the mother, Amalia, has a calming effect on her son. With her all-pardoning love, she anxiously and fearfully tries to still the terrible tempest in his soul. While Kamilla, the girl loved by both brothers, is a much more ineffectual and nebulous person, she too tries in her gentle way to dispel the gloom which hangs about the moody Guelfo.

Klinger has consciously created an eerie, sultry atmosphere for his drama to match its content. With the dark castle walls as a background which cuts off all communication with the outside world, the action is focused on the deep, foreboding twilight of the ancestral halls. Imitating Shakespeare and anticipating the "Schicksalsdramatiker" Werner and Müllner, Klinger, in the third act, uses a raging thunderstorm as a backdrop for Guelfo and Grimaldi, as they give vent to their frenzied emotions. Similarly, he uses fate symbols to portend a tragic outcome. The destruction of the orangery and of Ferdinando's favorite tree foreshadow the fate of the noble family, and of one of its members in particular.[19] Likewise the knell of the church bell in the night and the doleful lament of black-shrouded men bearing corpses are ominous signs.[20] When Klinger has a corpse on display in the final act, he follows the stage practice of Gerstenberg in *Ugolino*. The sight of the dead brother on a bier shakes Guelfo to the very depths, forcing him to confess his misdeeds and to face life honestly: "I killed him ... [Let] the avengers [come]! I have finished speaking."[21] This reminds us of Kaiser's Expressionistic drama *Die Bürger von Calais*, where viewing the dead hero has a similar purgative and regenerative effect on the characters.

The language of the drama is as violent, passionate, and gloomy as its setting and accurately reflects the temperaments of the main characters. Guelfo's speech and, on occasion, that of Grimaldi and the father, is uttered at a fever pitch to help convey the intensely passionate and emotional state of the protagonists. As an example of this explosive Storm and Stress style we quote Guelfo's soliloquy, spoken after he has had to face Kamilla and Amalia for the first time after Ferdinando's death. Revealing a man wavering between feelings of defiance, fear, remorse, and aversion, this emotion-packed speech is a good illustration of the powerful idiom which caught the fancy of the age:

Rächer! hi! hi! ich tat's wohl! Kömmt er noch nicht, mit glühender Hand den Mord einzugraben?—Ha! ich kann mich nicht ansehen! Reiss dich aus dir, Guelfo! Zerschlage dich Guelfo!—Guelfo! Guelfo! geh aus dir! Schaff dich um!—Jetzt will ich schlafen! O jetzt will ich sanft schlafen![22]

Avenger! heh! heh! I did it all right! Isn't he coming yet to bury the murder with a glowing hand? Ha! I can't bear to look at myself! Tear yourself away from yourself, Guelfo! Beat yourself up, Guelfo! Guelfo! Guelfo! Escape from yourself! Change yourself! Now I want to sleep! O now I want to sleep peacefully!

The verbal forms, which occupy a dominant position in this passage, convey intense physical and psychic activity and a need for urgent action. The concentration and repetition of words with great emotional recall serve to stimulate the ever increasing degree of passion. To further communicate a feeling of inner tension, the author places the most expressive word first in a sentence, disregards elemental rules of syntax, and connects phrases in incoherent sequences.

Contrasted to Guelfo's speech is that of the female characters, Amalia and Kamilla. In the following dialogue, Amalia, speaking in measured tones, reflects the lachrymal, sentimental, and passive nature of the eighteenth-century heroine: "And I and your father weep day and night over your rude nature. But I won't do it, my Guelfo, I will endure all, will endure it as a mother."[23] Such dialogue is quite similar to that of Miss Sara Sampson and Fräulein von Sternheim. Kamilla, and even the male characters, for the most part likewise use a calm, orderly, clear language, since they represent the overly refined, Rationalistic order, against which the primitive Guelfo revolts. Kurt May states that it is the mere presence of these coolly calculating yet effeminate counterfigures which incites the wild Guelfo to madness.[24]

An interesting question which we might pose here is: Just how wild and mad is Guelfo? H. B. Garland finds him "cold-bloodedly cruel and dominated by an enormous perverted vanity . . . a spoilt and ill-tempered child with all the dangerous strength of a grown man."[25] A contemporary of Klinger's, Gottfried August Bürger, reflects a similar point of view when he writes to a friend: "Guelfo is a beast whom I could enjoy seeing shot down as a mad dog. . . . There are, to be sure, more malicious rascals, but when they begin to become as mad and raving as Guelfo, the police puts them in chains."[26] In the Wilhelminian era, which often championed values of the Rationalistic age, Hettner wrote in kindred spirit, calling Die Zwillinge "a depiction of moral outrage, more tortuous and intolerable than the depiction of physical hunger pangs in Gerstenberg's Ugolino."[27] While these critical evaluations are true in part, they err in accepting Die Zwillinge, and especially the figure of Guelfo, at face value. We think that a clue to Klinger's real intent in writing this drama about a volcanic, emotional young man going berserk is provided in the letter quoted earlier.[28] Klinger writes to Schumann that he frequently experiences turbulent states of mind, but he is able, later on, to view this period of turmoil objectively and to laugh at himself. Seen in this light, *Die Zwillinge* does not have dangerous psychopathic implications, but is a healthy expression of those gloomy moods, which the author had to give vent to in order to regain his equilibrium. Klinger's drama caught the spirit of the age. In its convulsive and rash passions, it was the effective expression of a fermenting, restless spirit which pervaded contemporary youth. In his autobiographical novel *Anton Reiser*, Karl Philipp Moritz relates the effect which a theater performance of *Die Zwillinge* had on his hero: "Everything seemed to Reiser to be so true, as if lifted out of his own soul, which continually was filled with such dark fantasies, so that he imagined himself in the role of Guelfo, and for a time lived the part, adopting Guelfo's own thoughts and feelings."[29]

Another drama, written and published about the same time as *Die Zwillinge*, is Klinger's *Die neue Arria*. Here again the setting is an Italian court during the Renaissance, although the plot is taken from Plutarch's account of the brave wife of the Roman senator Paetus. The hero, Julio, revolts against the world in typical Klinger fashion, although it is not hostility between two brothers which instigates the emotional crisis, but rather the political intrigue in a corrupt court. The political goal—that of freeing a country from illegal and tyrannical control—is often lost sight of because of Klinger's greater interest in the fate of the lovers, Solina and Julio. Solina, a "Machtweib" in the true sense of the word, spurs on her weaker mate to heroic deeds, and when their mutual efforts in eradicating cancerous elements at the court fail, both commit suicide.

By effectively contrasting temperaments and personalities, Klinger heightens the dramatic tension. However, the feverish, exaggerated pitch of the dialogue creates an almost comic effect, since it does not emanate from a single wellspring of emotion, as in *Die Zwillinge*, but seems artificially contrived. Artistically inferior to the play about the hostile brothers, *Die neue Arria* nevertheless introduces motifs which occur in later dramas of Klinger.[30] *Die neue Arria* has also influenced works of other writers, especially Jean Paul's *Titan*. Linda and Albano, the superhuman figures in the latter novel, are patterned after Solina and Julio.

The heroes of Klinger's later dramas never attained the gloomy intensity of Guelfo's emotional outbursts, nor of those of Solina and Julio. The author himself seems to have reached a stage where he felt intuitively that it was time to contain his Storm and Stress spirit in order not to dissipate his talents, as Lenz had done, for example. In this connection, the young Klinger confirmed Goethe's evaluation of him, when the latter singled him out from the companions of his youth as the one who possessed a special degree of external and internal stability.[31] In the middle of these turbulent years, Klinger must have developed a desire to achieve self-control, a will to discipline himself, which allowed him to mature into a responsible and well-rounded individual. Artistically, this change manifests itself for the first time in the drama *Simsone Grisaldo*.

II Simsone Grisaldo

This drama was begun in the spring of 1776 in Giessen and very likely completed the same summer in Weimar. It is Klinger's changing and positive attitude toward the world and organized society which is at the core of all of the vital themes in *Simsone Grisaldo*. Although Klinger showed signs of maturing emotionally before he set foot in Weimar, it was the image of Goethe as a sober and responsible government official, which especially helped to temper him. In Goethe he experienced the true greatness of a man who lives true to himself but not for himself. A letter to Schleiermacher contains the pertinent remark: "Goethe is loved by all and is the salvation of the country. . . . He is involved in political affairs and has been beneficial to this country and does things."[32]

This enthusiasm for Goethe was even transferred to other celebrities in Weimar, especially to Wieland. The latter is termed "a terribly great and good man . . . who incorporates love, greatness, humility, and modesty."[33] The sterling qualities attributed to Goethe and Wieland are of particular interest to us, because they represent the characteristics which are imparted to the hero of the drama. Grisaldo may be viewed as an ideal of young Klinger, who earnestly yearns for inner harmony and a serene attitude toward the world. This desire for inner peace, in the spirit of Grisaldo, is expressed by Klinger in another letter to Schleiermacher: "And brother, it would be a characteristic of a great world spirit to have in one's heart the infinite sunrise, [to hear] the eternal song . . . and, besides, everything which I said and wanted to say in my Grisaldo."[34] Later on in the same letter, Klinger speaks of "Grisaldo's humility and love, which reflects my own nature more than you think." In Weimar, Klinger for the first time developed an appreciation for the busy, active life. When he says, "everybody is productive here," he approves of bustling, useful activity, just as Grisaldo does.

Simsone Grisaldo is important because it represents a significant milestone in the spiritual development of Klinger. Esthetically it is inferior to *Die Zwillinge* and *Sturm und Drang*, because it lacks unity of tone. Combining elements of the Commedia dell'arte, the baroque "Haupt- und Staatsaktionen," and the fairy-tale comedy with the serious Storm and Stress drama of social involvement, it has too many disparate parts to achieve artistic unity .

As the title of the drama implies, Simsone Grisaldo is the main character, through whom the play is held together. A strong, invincible soldier type, he is the victorious general of Castile, who conquers the Moors as well as the rebellious elements in Aragon. Originally a Sturm und Drang figure, who was "terrible in anger, frightful in rage, had all desires, and was intolerable,"[35] he was, however, also "helpful and good by nature."[36] Gradually, his qualities of kindness and altruism temper his spirit. Practicing rigorous self-discipline, he never entertains the idea of exploiting his powers; and after all his glorious military expeditions he bows down in humility before the weak and ungrateful king, subordinating his individual desires to the welfare of his countrymen.

Paradoxically enough, Grisaldo's noble personality awakens envy and jealousy in the hearts of some courtiers, who begin to plot against him. But he is unconcerned about the ingratitude and evil machinations of certain individuals, realizing that mankind cannot be changed. To his rhetorical questions: "Can I change the world? Make mankind better? . . . Change their hearts?",[37] he expects a negative answer. No blindly passionate Karl Moor who succumbs to pessimism, Grisaldo regards humble serving and patient endurance as his life's task and is finally rewarded at the end of the drama. The king as well as his enemies are won over by the power of his sympathetic feeling.

Through selfless love of mankind he has achieved inner harmony.
Reflecting the philosophy of Shaftesbury, he has become part of
the harmonious nature of the universe by effectively relating himself to his social responsibilities.[38]

If Grisaldo the soldier and statesman has learned to curb his
individual desires in the interest of others, this is not true of
Grisaldo the lover. The erotic and sensual facet of his personality
enjoys complete freedom. Following his uninhibited physical
urges, the "dark, curly-haired"[39] general courts a multitude of
women, and all are completely infatuated by him. There are,
above all, Almerine, the daughter of the Saracen king; Isabella,
the young noble lady of Aragon; Lilla, the pretty younger sister
of Bastiano; and her friend, the sentimental infanta. For Grisaldo
sensual love simply regenerates man physically and is the privilege of the strong, exceptional individual. In no way are
Grisaldo's adventures in love depicted in the gay and frivolous
spirit of the Rococo age; rather, in line with Rousseau's gospel
of nature, they are represented as natural expressions and experiences of a free and powerful person. Klinger is clearly further-
ing a new morality for the tradition-bound eighteenth century,
which is to replace the outmoded and hypocritical practices of a
decadent society.

In his love affair with Almerine, Simsone Grisaldo exhibits the
same superhuman and overly sensual characteristics as his prototype and namesake from the Bible, Samson. Even the biblical
motif of the strength inherent in his hair occurs in the idyllic,
fairy-tale-like scene, where Grisaldo spends a night with Almerine in the grotto (I, 3). Almerine ties her hair into a knot with
those of her lover, and he throws his sword away so as to be
completely in the power of his "sorceress." But Almerine wants
a strong hero, undoes the knot and returns the sword, thus sym-
bolizing her intent to submit and renounce. In her words:
"Woman is to inflame the hero but not weaken him."[40] Later on,
Almerine rescues Grisaldo from his enemies, and it is because of
her unselfish and sacrificial nature that she becomes Grisaldo's
favorite.

We are led to believe that the other women friends, passionate and compliant though they may be, are less successful in
permanently winning Grisaldo's love, because they entertain egotistical desires. Isabella, the young and spirited lady of Aragon,

is captivated by his powerful eyes, and with ardent kisses drinks life and rapture from his lips.[41] But in her feverish efforts to possess him she twice betrays her dashing hero. Her intrigues, which do not stop short of fomenting a war between two rival states in order that Grisaldo, as general, will be obliged to come to her castle, are reminiscent of the high adventure of the Baroque "Haupt- und Staatsaktionen." In common with the latter type of drama are also the scenes of the lovers' rescue from the burning castle and Isabella's treacherous and revengeful efforts to blind her errant suitor and take him captive.

In Grisaldo's amourous adventures with Lilla and the infanta, a lighter tone is injected into the drama, and Grisaldo's seductive powers are parodied. Lilla, the gay, lively, and coquettish sister of Bastiano, flits about the palace gardens, playing a merry game of hide-and-seek with her knightly hero. In her mischievous pranks, as when she pelts the infanta's pesky suitor with oranges and lemons, she adopts the antics of contemporary popular comedy. Around her flippant and superficial personality centers the gay interlude which is injected in this basically serious drama.

The infanta, too, appears in the scenes of lighter vein, although she is much more sentimental than her friend Lilla. At the mercy of her instincts, as are all the characters, with the exception of Grisaldo and his evil adversaries, she is intuitively drawn to the natural goodness of Grisaldo as opposed to the hypocritical and feigned ardor of her other suitors: Curio, Bastiano, and Zifaldo.

From the foregoing discussion it is apparent that Klinger employs Baroque contrasts to achieve dramatic effect, just as he did in *Die Zwillinge*. Scenes, characters, moods, and manners are set off against each other. Playing the role of a dangerous antagonist to the ideal Grisaldo is Bastiano, the aristocratic son of Don Fernando. Although he is blessed with superior physical and mental powers and limitless passion and ambition, as is Grisaldo, he lacks the latter's altruistic motives, being altogether an opportunistic individualist. In his words: "I am alone in the world, I am in the world for my advantage."[42] By contrasting two extraordinary men who are quantitatively but not qualitatively alike, Klinger anticipates, with Grisaldo and Bastiano, similar figures in Jean Paul's *Titan* (Albano and Roquairol) and in Ibsen's *Crown Pretenders* (Hakon and Skule). Like his antagonist, Bastiano follows his erotic instincts, but he is primarily interested in the polit-

ical gain which will accrue from his amorous adventures. His
political-erotic strategy, which is to gain the crown of Castile by
winning the infanta's heart, goes awry when Curio, likewise a
suitor of the infanta, thwarts his plans. In a jealous mood Bastiano expresses his love in convulsive fashion:

Castilien! Aragonien! Leon! Deine schneeweisse Hand! Deine Lilien-
hand! Dein weisser gehobner Busen! Dein elfenbeinerer Hals! Deine
spielenden, schlimmen Augen! Deine blonden schönen Bogen obenü-
ber! Die Röte deiner Wangen! Deine Haare den Nacken herunter—
bist du auf meinen Lippen, Seele? Willst du ausspannen, Geist? Und
ich atme und ziehe dich zurück und geissle dich Unbändigen, schrei
und tobe! Bastiano, über dir![43]

Castile! Aragon! Leon! Your snow white hand! Your lily white hand!
Your high white bosom! Your neck of ivory! Your playful, evil eyes!
Your beautiful, blonde arches above them! Your red cheeks! Your long
hair around your neck. Are you on my lips, O soul? Do you want to
give me release, spirit? And I breathe and pull you back and bind you
who can't be bound, I cry and rave! Bastiano, beyond you!

The passage above, with its flowery expletives and bombastic
and extravagant mannerisms, is reminiscent of Baroque drama.
The quote is particularly significant, since it marks a striking exception to the style of the drama in general, which is written in
a much more subdued and realistic language than *Die Zwillinge,*
in keeping with Klinger's maturing attitude toward life.

In the end, all of Bastiano's machinations employed to unhorse
Grisaldo are unsuccessful, and the latter magnanimously spares
his life. If the role of Bastiano is conceived to be, at least pre-
dominantly, a serious one, those of his two accomplices, Curio
and Truffaldino, are only to be regarded humorously. All three
men have the same aspirations, and their actions develop into a
contest of three fools who try mutually to outwit one another
(III, 1). Their intrigues reach a peak in the grotesque scene
(V, 2) in which they vie for the throne and lose everything. As
mentioned before, the coquettish Lilla plays a key role in this
comic buffoonery; at night she has a masked band "pinch, annoy,
beat, and scratch"[44] her lovesick suitor, the pedantic Curio, who
reminds us of Falstaff. His most pronounced character trait is
that of great sensual passion, which, in his early days, he sought
to sublimate by engaging in scholarly activity and by writing
sentimental poetry.

In the figure of Curio, Klinger ridicules the heartless and fictitious sentimental poetry, which only a man without power and true feeling is able to write. Love for the infanta gradually frees him from all inhibitions and releases all his feelings, so that he hurls himself into the thicket, groans, and runs around like a madman.[45] Unfortunately, because of his decadence he is so weakened in mind and in body that he is ineffective as a lover and as a statesman. A grotesque figure, he gets to look like a skeleton,[46] his temples being hollow, his face sunken, and his eyes dull and lifeless.[47] Although both he and Bastiano have similar sensual and passionate natures, Curio lacks the strength and willpower of his accomplice.

The third member of the notorious trio, Truffaldino, is a comic theatrical figure, whom Klinger borrowed from the Commedia dell'arte. A court astrologer of humble origin, whose vanity and ambition cause him to aspire to the crown, he is the least harmless among the caricatures of courtiers. Banned from the court along with the other conspirators, he appears in the last scene of the play content to wear a fool's cap. At the close, he expounds his "new" philosophy: "Man, cultivate your garden and remain within your limits, outside is storm and wind."[48] In Truffaldino's transformation, the author very likely reveals the compromise he himself had to strike between his high ideals and the sober insights of reality.

A most interesting comic creation, who is a product of diverse literary influences, is Zifaldo, the Saracen prince. As a primitive, whom we have come to recognize as a favorite of the age, he owes much to Rousseau. The author of *Emile* would have admired him for being untainted by civilization and for possessing all of his healthy, natural powers. But he is also a spiritual kin of Prince Tandi, the representative of the exotic primitive country in Lenz's *Der neue Menoza*. Like Tandi he is the outsider who is able to view European culture objectively and is appalled by what he sees. On comparing the two dramas in general, we must mention that *Simsone Grisaldo* shares with *Menoza* the same fairy-tale atmosphere and comic characters of the Commedia dell'arte type; and like Lenz in his dramas, *Grisaldo* employs a loose, disjointed plot and copious stage directions, which are often used to indicate significant gestures.

On comparing the characters of Prince Tandi and Zifaldo in

more detail, we must admit that they also exhibit noteworthy differences. Prince Tandi is cast as a serious, idealized figure who philosophizes on an esoteric plane about life in Europe, while Zifaldo offers comic relief as a goodnatured barbarian who operates purely by instinct and admires the Spaniards who do likewise. At the mercy of his erotic impulses, he is a spirited young stud who no sooner sees Lilla,[49] the infanta,[50] and Isabella,[51] than he wants to sleep with them. Although Zifaldo's energetic and honest nature, as well as his disgust with a hypocritical civilization, are extolled by Klinger, he is the butt of laughter, because he cannot control his sensual urges. In his negative depiction of Zifaldo, Klinger clearly shows that he is outgrowing Storm and Stress individualism, where man is guided solely by his feelings. Showing the influence of Shaftesbury, Klinger wants his heroes to temper their personal desires in the interest of the common good and thereby attain a harmonious personality.

This trend toward moderation is reflected in the mood and style of the drama. Except for the bombastic outbursts of Bastiano and his accomplices,[52] the characters in general speak in a more measured cadence. To be sure, some of the personages still occasionally use picturesque speech which appears, at first glance, to be the expression of an individual who is overcome by his passions and compelled to use language to fit his dire emotional state. By way of example, Curio "runs back and forth in the garden, and sighs to the stars,"[53] and "bites out his teeth, and bites off his tongue."[54] Zifaldo has "perpetrated a terrible bloodbath while lion hunting,"[55] and his father advises him to "howl to the winds, so that the bowels of the earth tremble."[56] Bastiano finds relief by "running about at night and biting his fingers,"[57] and Grisaldo loosens emotional tension by "shaking himself and roaring like a lion."[58] But in each of the above instances the circumstances do not warrant such effusive language; rather, these excesses in diction seem to be a fad on Klinger's part, a vestige of those turbulent days when he created *Die Zwillinge*.

To a certain extent, the bombast also serves as an element of parody. In this drama, where Grisaldo's serious discussions with Malvizino about affairs of state alternate with the ridiculous machinations of Truffaldino, it is understandable that the language should reflect the caricatured personalities as well as those treated more respectfully. Artistically, *Simsone Grisaldo* is an interesting and highly original composition, in which power and Eros, superman and his parody are intertwined in bewildering fashion. In Klinger's pioneering efforts to infuse into the conventional drama elements of the Baroque theater, the Commedia dell'arte, and the exotic fairy tale, he has created a work in which the characters are so poorly motivated and which is so loosely connected that it is almost impossible to find a unifying thread. Still, the drama is rich in poetic fantasy and did serve as a testing ground for the more esthetically pleasing *Sturm und Drang*, where the alternation of serious and parodistic elements is carried out in a more consistent and effective manner. From the standpoint of the author's spiritual development, *Simsone Grisaldo* is a milestone. Through the character of the central figure, Klinger reveals his progress in attaining clarity and in coping with the human condition.

III Sturm und Drang

Klinger had originally given this drama the title "Wirrwarr," but at the behest of Christoph Kaufmann, the notorious apostle of Lavater's doctrines whom Maler Müller caricatured in his *Faust*,[59] it was published under the name of *Sturm und Drang*. The new title became a catchword, and before long it was used to designate the entire literary movement brought into being by the geniuses of the 1770's.

If *Simsone Grisaldo* revealed an author who was maturing emotionally and adjusting to life's problems, the next work, *Sturm und Drang*, must be interpreted as an artistic creation of a man who suffered a temporary relapse in his spiritual development. Indeed, the summer and fall of 1776, when Klinger wrote *Sturm und Drang*, marked a time of serious crisis. On arriving in Weimar in June, he was elated to be a part of the select court society, presided over by Goethe, whom he admired especially for having achieved balance of character through his varied responsibilities in state affairs. It was not long, however, before Klinger, a scion of the most humble social class, felt ill at ease in the courtly, patrician atmosphere. He soon perceived that in the small capital town "today is like yesterday, and yesterday is like today."[60] A longing for the "vita activa" beset him, and he played with the idea of pursuing an officer's career, "the only profession in which one can keep his force of spirit and strength of character, and resign one's self the least."[61] To seek clarity Klinger planned to fight in the American Revolution under the British flag.[62] Another idea he entertained was to become an actor, "which could satisfy everything."[63]

It was during this state of consternation, when he was undecided as to how to employ his talents, that he had an altercation with Goethe, which resulted in his leaving Weimar, to which he was never to return. In these restless days and months, when his life "began to be wild and diffuse,"[64] he conceived and wrote the drama *Sturm und Drang*. In a letter to Schleiermacher, dated September 4, 1776, Klinger mentions the new play: "I am writing a comedy of confusion [Wirrwarr], which is almost finished. . . . I have brought together the wildest eccentrics. And the deepest tragic feeling alternates with laughing and neighing."[65]

The dramatic action of the play takes place at an inn in America during the Revolutionary War days, although the milieu, in typical Klinger fashion, is depicted so vaguely that one could never identify the locale without the author specifically stating it. The plot, in essence, runs as follows: two English noblemen, Lord Bushy and Lord Berkley, have become mortal enemies after enjoying years of the closest friendship. But Bushy's son, called "Wild," a prototype of the typical tempestuous Storm and Stress "Kraftmensch," secretly loves Berkley's daughter, Jenny Karoline, and after endless wanderings finally finds her in America. By virtue of their mutual love, and with the aid of absurdities and unmotivated actions on the part of their friends and acquaintances, the two families are reunited at the end.

Wild has brought with him to America two friends, La Feu and Blasius, whose characterizations and experiences form the core of a humorously conceived subplot. La Feu, a sentimental poet who lives in a world of illusions, finds his female counterpart among the courtly relatives of Berkley. Blasius, likewise a parody figure, is a distraught youth with melancholy inclinations, who solves life's problems by becoming a hermit. The minor characters serve to dramatize the conflicting moods of Klinger's time and of his own personality.

Again, as in *Die Zwillinge* and *Simsone Grisaldo*, Klinger employs a central figure—in this case Wild—to express his personal feelings, especially his revolt against the world. Wild, endowed with a passionate temperament and rich intuitive sense, has lost his equanimity because the enmity between the Berkley and Bushy families has caused him to lose his loved one (Jenny Karoline) and his home. Forced to leave his close friends and even his fatherland, he wanders in a confused state of mind from one country to another. In order to soothe his tormented soul he lives in the Alps and tends goats in Rousseauean fashion; he goes to fight in wars in Russia and Spain, and when war fails to materialize in the latter country, he comes to America, in order that "his soul can distend itself."[66] Completely frustrated and filled with pent-up emotions he makes his famous drum-and-pistol speech: "I want to be stretched over a drum, in order to get a new dimension. I feel sick at heart again. If I could only exist within the range of this pistol, until a hand exploded me into the air."[67]

Although Wild is at the lowest ebb here, his language is not uttered at a fever pitch, nor spoken with the violent intensity of Guelfo in *Die Zwillinge*. In *Sturm und Drang*, Klinger's characters rarely speak in incoherent sentence fragments, and ejaculatory expressions are kept to a minimum. To be sure, the turbulence of Klinger's latter Weimar days is reflected in the new drama, so that some of Wild's effusive protestations and pessimistic views must be taken at face value. But the author, who gave signs of shedding his Storm and Stress cloak in *Simsone Grisaldo*, is already parodying the spirit and mannerisms of the age of genius in the antics and language of his characters.

In all of Klinger's dramas written during the 1770's the roaring and frenzied gesticulations of the characters was more bark than bite; the naïve revolt of youth with its bombastic utterances was often little more than a kicking over of the traces and served therapeutic ends. *Sturm und Drang* accentuates this tendency. Klinger's remark to Schleiermacher, mentioned above, that the deepest tragic feeling alternates with laughing and neighing, achieves new significance. That is, by effectively blending the agonized struggles of the hero with elements of burlesque, the author has devised an artistic method which effectively expressed his innermost feelings.

After Wild's tragicomic drum-and-pistol speech, his outlook on life gradually brightens, with the first impetus for change coming from his discovering Karoline at the inn. But as in the case of Guelfo in *Die Zwillinge*, in his central role he is subjected to a series of catastrophic situations, which cause him to express himself in paroxysms of emotion. Setting off the main crises are his confrontation with Berkley, paradoxically both his enemy and the father of his beloved; his realization that the sea captain he hates intuitively is Karoline's brother; and a shocking (although false) report that the captain has killed Wild's father. To purge himself of his hate and his violent passions, Wild uses his old recipe: taking part in a battle. After one day at the front, he regains his self-confidence and firmness (V, 5), although it is his and Karoline's unwavering love for each other which finally removes all discord.

Karoline, Lord Berkley's beautiful and charming daughter, who is closely attuned to nature and her intuitive powers, is the poet's feminine ideal, and as such she is the character who is least parodied. Given to sadness and fits of melancholy in the period before she regains Wild's love, she gradually develops a serenity of character, a trait which Klinger extols in women. The Karoline-Wild love story obviously borrows several themes from Shakespeare's *Romeo and Juliet*. When these two lovers were separated, they were thirteen and fifteen—the same ages as their counterparts in the English play; the enmity of their houses keeps the lovers apart; and a moonlit balcony scene is reminiscent of Shakespeare, although it takes on a grotesque aspect when Wild climbs a tree in order to be able to speak more intimately to Karoline in the upstairs window (III, 8).

As we have noted in the two dramas previously discussed, Klinger employs contrast, especially of temperament and personality, to add to the dramatic effect. This method is also used in *Sturm und Drang*. The feuding fathers, Bushy and Berkley—the names obviously derive from Shakespeare's *Richard II*—are studies in opposites. Lord Bushy, who in his youth combines passionate feeling with physical and spiritual strength (just as his son Wild does), has been mellowed by time into a kindly old man of gentle feelings, who wants to live in peace with his enemies and his fellow citizens.

As such he represents the greatest contrast to Lord Berkley, who reveals his true nature in the first scene in which he appears (I, 2). His passionate soul is filled with hate for the Bushy fam-

ily, as he builds a house of cards and then destroys it, in re-
membrance of his lost happiness. Although the reason for the
hostility between the two clans is poorly delineated, it seems that
a third party, never mentioned by name, has fanned the fires of
discord and jealously for his own advantage and has provoked
Bushy to attack his former friend. At midnight, Bushy sacks and
burns Berkley's castle, and in the aftermath Berkley's wife is
dead and his son is missing. Only his daughter remains (I, 2). In
the action of the drama, Berkley exists in a state of confusion,
alternating between quiet, subdued interludes when in the company of his daughter, and hate-filled violent moments in which
he plans revenge. The latter moods predominate, and the angry
tirades reach such heights of bombastic rhetoric that they border
on the comically grotesque. A typically Baroque extravagance is
found in the curse he puts on Bushy: "May his hair become pierc-
ing snakes, and the fibers of his heart change to scorpions."[68] A
succession of events—discovering that the captain is his long-lost
son; taking part in a battle; observing Karoline's and Bushy's
mutual concern for one another; and especially Lord Bushy's
self-effacing attempts at reconciliation—gradually cause Berkley
to overcome his rage and regain his equilibrium.

The characters of La Feu and Blasius serve both to parody
character traits which Klinger found undesirable and to blend
the tragic and comic aspects of the drama. By contrasting the
two personages—with Wild on the one hand, and with their lady
friends, Aunt Kathrin and Luise, on the other—Klinger has created most interesting and eccentric personalities.

La Feu, whose name is taken from Shakespeare's *All's Well
That Ends Well*, is repelled by reality and, following Truffaldino's advice in *Simsone Grisaldo*, transforms the unsatisfactory
actual world into a beautiful dream with the aid of his supersensitive powers of imagination. Instead of facing the harsh mundane world head-on with all his powers and strength, as does
Wild, he prefers to live in a world of illusion. At the American
inn, where the Berkley retinue is staying, he meets his ideal in
Aunt Kathrin. The latter, a genuine product of the Rococo age,
with its courtly society which indulges in courteous but idle
pleasantries, feels totally misplaced in the primitive atmosphere
of America. Imagining that she is young and the desirable companion of gay cavaliers, she is attracted to La Feu, who likewise

has fashioned for himself a dream world of fantastic fairy tales and pastoral poetry.

Kathrin, as a sensitive, but sickly and rather ugly old maid who is plagued by coughing and sneezing (I, 4), and La Feu, whose "sweet, blonde hair" Kathrin raves about (although in reality he is wearing a brick-red wig), form a grotesque couple. They appear especially ridiculous in a moonlit garden scene (III, 6) where they pledge their undying love for each other. In their last appearance (V, 3) they decide to retreat from life as an Arcadian shepherd and shepherdess under the names of Phyllis and Damon. There is one final paradoxical twist. The sensual aunt, who has set all her hopes on marriage, has to be satisfied with a "spiritual" and "fantastic" relationship.[69] Doutbless Klinger employs the La Feu and Kathrin episode to ridicule literature of the Rococo, pastoral mode, and to parody the Romantic artist who lacks the strength to cope with the human condition. Rieger suggests that La Feu and Blasius are additional masks of Klinger himself, which the author wants to expose to criticism.[70]

The character of Blasius reminds us of Grimaldi in *Die Zwillinge*. True to his name, he is thoroughly bored with life and indifferent to it, after leading a varied and adventurous existence with his two companions, Wild and La Feu. Originally a man who acted in harmony with his emotional instincts, he is so buffeted about by the vicissitudes of life that he is only an empty shell of his former person and becomes melancholy and self-centered in his desperation. He has a strong yearning for nothingness: "I am again nothing at all, and want to be nothing."[71] He is apathetic, cannot dance or carry on a conversation, and yet he is drawn to women, because "they amount to so little and I to nothing at all."[72]

In the niece of Lord Berkley, Luise, he finds a companion in nullity. Lacking sensuality and genuine feeling, Luise is a coquettish and superficial girl. Because a genuine individual like Wild intuitively resists her advances, she makes overtures to Blasius as a last resort. Rivaling La Feu and Kathrin in grotesqueries, Blasius and Luise can scarcely tolerate each other. On a walk with her in the moonlight, Blasius has to sit down and feels sick (III, 9); on another occasion in the drawing room, Luise beats Blasius with her fan in hopes of getting him to react (II, 2). Blasius even has the impertinence to suggest marriage:

"We are ideally suited for it. Because, when we are together, I am bored and Miss is bored. To create this condition and to tolerate it is part of marriage."[73] But on second thought, and in all seriousness, Blasius decides to retreat alone to a cave and become a hermit, leaving the irritated and frustrated Luise in the lurch (V, 4).

Rieger suggests that Blasius reflects the author's personal moods; since in his letters Klinger reveals himself, at times, as a despondent, melancholy young man who revels in his fantasies.[74] Klinger, who at this stage of his development was searching for a solution to his youthful confusion, naturally wants to parody the Blasius figure. As a forerunner of similar types in German literature, Blasius also deserves mention. As Brüggemann points out, he prefigures Tieck's Lovell and Jean Paul's Roquairol as a character who becomes bored and very tired of his existence.[75] At a later date, Blasius' counterpart appears as Büchner's prince in *Leonce und Lena* and as the captain in *Wozzek.*

In contrast to the caricatured personalities above, who suffer from overexposure to civilization, the Moorish boy appears as a refreshing change. Except for lacking his erotic instincts, he has much in common with Prince Zifaldo. Though a primitive, he is endowed with a natural gentility and an elemental love for mankind which wins him the respect of the captain and Lord Bushy and helps to bring about the final reconciliation of the families. He is generally treated as a human being and as an equal, regardless of the fact that he enters the action of the play as a black slave. Klinger casts him in a favorable light, primarily because he possesses a rich store of sensitive, intuitive feelings on a primitive level, untainted by decadent society.

For the sake of completeness, the Moorish boy's master, Captain Boyet—who is in reality Berkley's son—is worthy of note. In Klinger's scheme of contrasts, the captain is paired off with Wild. Both are men of fierce passions and deep feeling, and both suffer unjustly in the quarrels of their houses. While Wild's frustrated emotions are gradually tempered by love, the captain's torment expresses itself in hate, allowing his nobility of nature to take a rude, hideous, degenerate turn. But in the optimistic conclusion even the captain is searching for harmony within himself, which will aid him in developing a more congenial social posture.

The alternation of the captain's spiteful tirades with the play's conciliatory moods forms an integral part of the dramatic technique. As Hering correctly concludes, the esthetic use of contrasts gives *Sturm und Drang* its peculiar style. The sublime and the vulgar, the serious and the ridiculous, the intimate and the cosmic, feeling and cold reason, all appear as polar opposites. In juxtaposing fiercely passionate moods with soothing lyrical ones, in depicting a wide range of feelings in their subtle nuances, Klinger sought to catch the essence of Shakespearean spirit.[76] As we have noted, the author uses individuals dissimilar in temperament and Weltanschauung to exemplify the contrasting emotional states, but at times a character is a psychological complexity in himself.

The language of the characters forms an integral part of their personalities and, in keeping with the tenor of the drama, assumes a wide variety of aspects. We have previously illustrated the bombastic tirades of Wild and Berkley, which occur in the earlier stages of the drama. In the very first scene, La Feu as well expresses his frustrations in crude baroque extravagances:

In the name of Amor! I want to fall in love with an old woman, live in an old dilapidated house, bathe my delicate body in a stinking manure puddle to curb my fantasy. Is there no old witch around, with whom I could flirt? Her wrinkles would become wavy lines of beauty; her protruding black teeth would become marble columns for Diana's temple; her drooping leather tits would surpass Helena's bosoms.[77]

But such wildly emotional outbursts, replete with grotesque images, occur infrequently, and then only in the first acts. Of more significance in La Feu's speech are the allusions to the Rococo spirit (references to classical mythology; a dream of an ideal world of fantasy; the coquettish word "scharmieren"), for a parodistic Rococo style sets the tone of the play. In those instances where the characters use an affected and overly refined speech, Klinger is satirizing certain individuals and the culture they represent. Sometimes, under the influence of nature, an individual appears unparodied, speaking a soft, fluid language, which reflects a harmonious personality. In this respect, Wild's soliloquy, spoken in the moonlit garden in the third act, is quite typical:

Die Nacht liegt so kühl, so gut um mich! Die Wolken ziehen so still dahin! Ach sonst, wie alles trüb und düster war! Wohl, mein Herz! dass du dies Schauerhafte wieder einmal rein fühlen kannst! dass die Nachtlüftchen dich umsäuseln und du die Liebe wehen fühlst in der ganzen stillen Natur.[78]

Night feels so cool, so good around me! The clouds move by so quietly! Oh, how melancholy and gloomy everything was before! It is well, my heart, that you can experience fully again this feeling of awe; that the night breezes waft about you, and that you can hear the murmur of love in the vast stillness of nature.

The quotation just cited is indicative of the play's positive intent. In spite of some tempestuous, tragicomic involvements, the main characters gradually develop an inner firmness, enabling them to view life optimistically. Karl Bushy, alias Wild, follows the advice that old Guelfo gave his son by taking part in battle to soothe his frustrated passions. And Karl, in marked contrast to the hero of *Die Zwillinge,* wins Karoline's hand at the end, thus obtaining what he prized most. Symbolically, Klinger is showing that he is gradually overcoming his youthful eccentricities and is well on the way toward acquiring self-assurance and self-control. His next drama, *Stilpo und seine Kinder,* written in 1777 and published in 1780, is no longer within the Storm and Stress orbit. Although powerful passions still come to the fore, they no longer rage, and wild and crude elements are supplanted by a generally more reserved atmosphere. Klinger is entering his "Weltmann und Dichter" phase, which came to fruition during his years in Russia.

CHAPTER 6

Johann Anton Leisewitz:
A Traditionalist Flirts with Genius

O F THE Storm and Stress dramatists, Leisewitz is the only one who did not come directly under Goethe's influence. His literary career was also the least productive, for he is remembered only for one play, *Julius von Tarent*. Always mentioned in connection with Klinger's *Zwillinge*, with which it was entered in competition, Leisewitz' play shares the same theme of fratricide and the same emphasis on the tragic implications of demonic passion. But in its construction it shows much more deliberation and restraint than does Klinger's work, reflecting the personality of the author.

Leisewitz was born in Hannover in 1752, the son of a prosperous wine merchant. After attending the local "Gymnasium," where he developed an admiration for Lessing's works, he matriculated at the university of Göttingen in 1770 to study law. Culturally, Göttingen was dominated at this time by the "Hainbund," and on July 2, 1774, at Klopstock's birthday celebration, Leisewitz officially became a member of this literary group. He speaks of Voss, Miller, Bürger, and the Stolberg brothers,[1] but of all the members of the "Hainbund" he seems to have had the closest relationship with Hölty. A shy, retiring hypochondriac, Leisewitz felt a natural kinship to the gentle-mannered, melancholy, and sickly Hölty and personally cared for him during the last weeks of his life. The depiction of nature, the graveyard atmosphere, and the extreme sentimentality in some of the scenes of *Julius von Tarent* show a kinship to the poetry of the "Hainbund" and of Hölty in particular.

In his first year at the university, Leisewitz became personally acquainted with Lessing, who was the librarian in nearby Wolfenbüttel. The two men became fast friends, especially after the appearance in 1776 of *Julius von Tarent*, which Lessing praised most highly. After leaving Göttingen in the fall of 1774 Leisewitz returned to his native Hannover to practice law. But most of his time was occupied by literary activity, and under the stimulating influence of Hölty and new friends such as Ebert, Eschenburg, Gärtner, and Zachariae, he wrote two poetic dialogues (*Die Pfändung* and *Der Besuch um Mitternacht*) in 1775 and his only completed drama.

In the early 1770's, Leisewitz busied himself with Voltaire and Montaigne and with Shakespeare, Pope, and Shaftesbury.[2] In a letter to his future wife, Sophie Seyler, the daughter of Abel Seyler of theater fame, he calls Rousseau his favorite author.[3] There can be no doubt that Leisewitz, abreast of the comtempo-rary literary scene as he was, knew the works of young Goethe. Both men had mutual friends in the Stolberg brothers, but the two did not meet personally until August, 1780, when Leisewitz visited Weimar. Goethe's only comment on the visit is a terse entry in his diary: "Leisewitz was here for a few days."[4] In Weimar, Leisewitz made a favorable impression on Herder, with whom he had carried on a correspondence in earlier years, and to whom he had given the manuscript of *Julius von Tarent* even before entering it in the competition.[5]

After spending four years in Hannover as a lawyer, Leisewitz took a position with the government in Braunschweig, where he remained for the rest of his life. His writing practically ceased. He had set himself the task of writing a history of the Thirty Years' War, but when Schiller's work on the same subject ap-peared, he destroyed the manuscript. At his death in 1806, in deference to his wishes, all his papers, including a comedy, *Die Weiber von Weinsberg*, were burned. Hettner, basing his theory on Leisewitz' reaction to the publication of Schiller's monumen-tal historical work, surmises that Leisewitz' creative activity suf-fered because, measured against Goethe and Schiller, he felt his talents were wanting.[6]

Of the extant literary works besides *Julius von Tarent*, only the poetic dialogues are worthy of note. Two scenes from the con-templated tragedies "Konradin" and "Alexander und Hephästion" appeared in the July, 1776, issue of Boie's *Deutsches Museum*, but they are too fragmentary to warrant discussion. The poetic dialogues, *Die Pfändung* and *Der Besuch um Mitternacht*, which appeared in the *Göttinger Musenalmanach* of 1775,[7] bear the stamp of the "Hainbund" in spirit and content. Love of freedom, hate for tyrannical oppression, love of fatherland, and a naïve belief in immortality are motifs which permeate both prose dialogues, each of which is one scene in length. In *Die Pfändung* the two principals are a peasant and his wife sleeping in their bedroom for the last time before their possessions are seized by officers of the Prince. Both comfort each other with the thought that their bed may be taken from them, but not their immortality. Though social criticism is not overtly expressed, it is implied through irony and understatement. Leisewitz' talent for reproducing the speech and milieu of the common people reminds us of Lenz and Wagner.

In *Der Besuch um Mitternacht*, the indignation over the corruption of state and society is more explicit. At midnight, in Shakespearean fashion, the ghost of Arminius appears before the Prince, who is actually expecting his mistress. Rebuking the tyrant Prince for making slaves of his subjects and for being a slave of a whore, Arminius prophesies the end of despotism and the dawn of freedom. This antagonism to political institutions is expressed, once more, in *Julius von Tarent*, Leisewitz' only completed play.

I   Julius von Tarent

Although this drama was published for the first time in 1776, there is evidence that Leisewitz had begun writing it in 1771 and had produced a finished version in September, 1774.[8] Contrary to Klinger's method of completing his dramas in feverish haste, Leisewitz worked slowly and deliberately and rewrote various scenes. There are amazing similarities in theme and plot between *Julius von Tarent* and *Die Zwillinge*, but it is fruitless to delve into the problem of plagiarizing, since each drama, in the final analysis, reflects the distinctive style of the author. Suffice it so say that Leisewitz wrote most of his play before Klinger started on his.

Julius von Tarent is based on a tale about Duke Cosimo I of Florence and his sons, although Leisewitz moved the locale to Tarento, substituted the local ruling house for the Medici, and took liberties with characters and events to suit his particular needs. As in Klinger's play, two sons of widely different temperaments love the same girl. But where Klinger makes the strong, ambitious man of action his hero, Leisewitz builds his drama around the older brother, Julius, who is a gentle, sentimental, introspective Werther type. Julius loves Blanca with such a passion that he is willing to give up his rights as firstborn to the throne, while the younger brother Guido will not renounce his love for the girl, because his honor would not tolerate it. In an effort to placate his sons, the Prince of Tarento has Blanca removed to a convent, and he enlists the Countess Caecilia to try to win Julius' affection. These diversionary tactics fail, mainly because Julius will not be put off. When the latter embarks on a plan to kidnap Blanca, Guido hears of the ruse, intercepts his brother, and stabs him to death. The father, in his role as ruler of the state, administers justice by killing Guido.

In this drama, Leisewitz has combined Lessing's dramatic structure and language with Storm and Stress motifs to fashion a stageworthy play. Unimpressed by the non-Aristotelian methods of Lenz, Leisewitz begins his drama on one morning and ends it on the next, has the action take place in the palace or the convent, and limits the number of characters. The play begins with a masterful exposition, which culminates in a climax midway in the third act. Except for the Caecilia episode, there is no digression of any kind, and each of the five acts has seven scenes on the average. Most of the scenes are built around a dialogue of two persons.

From the title it is obvious that Julius will occupy most of our attention. In the very first scene of the play, he appears to us as a sensitive young man, a sentimental dreamer:

As I enter my room at night, the moon darts in a few beams, and they fall on Blanca's picture. I look at it, and it seems to me as though her face is distorting itself for weeping, and a moment later I saw bright pearls roll down her cheeks. It was fantasy, but fantasy that could make me suspicious of all reality.[9]

His father notes that he answers "like one whose soul is far away."[10] Completely absorbed in his daydreams, he feels incompetent to make rational decisions, which task he delegates to his friend Aspermonte. Only intuitive feeling holds sway over him. He bases his friendship with Aspermonte on feeling, as well as his love for Blanca. Because he fears that the free exercise of his natural feelings will be curbed some day when he takes over

the reins of government as his father's legal successor, he seeks to
shake his externally imposed responsibilities. Wishing to exchange power and fame for closeness to nature, he says, "Give
me but one field in return for my principality and a babbling
brook for a cheering populace."[11]

In his antagonism to the state as a political instiution, Julius
furthers the views of Rousseau. When Aspermonte reminds him
anew of his obligations, he allows his emotions to speak out
against the existing social order:

And must the whole human race, in order to be happy, be locked up
in states, where each is a slave of the other, and no one is free—where
each is riveted to the other end of the chain by which he holds his
slaves fast? Only idiots can argue whether society poisons mankind—
both sides admit that the state kills freedom.[12]

The freedom that Julius seeks is not freedom within the law, but
freedom from law. Instead of the fetters of society, he demands
the feeling of freedom and of love—"a love which in its infinite
way embraces all of humanity as a cosmic emotion."[13] In the lines
quoted above, Leisewitz depicts the unease of man in modern
society. Julius feels an irreconcilable antagonism between his
inner values and the external social forms, just as Lenz's Hofmeister and Müller's Faust did.

The political and humanitarian conversations between Julius
and Aspermonte remind us of those between Schiller's Don
Carlos and Marquis Posa. Aspermonte, the prototype of Posa,
is the unselfish, loyal friend, although he is not depicted as carefully and fully as Schiller's character. Schiller, who was enthralled by *Julius* in his youth, admits that "the blood and nerves
of Carlos are those of Leisewitz's Julius."[14]

From the standpoint of the brother conflict, Julius and Guido
most decidedly influenced the brothers Moor of *Die Räuber*. In
both dramas, one brother loves the girl passionately and sin-
cerely; the other merely wants the girl as a symbol of honor and
conquest. The comparison of the two sets of brothers may not
be carried too far, however, because Karl Moor incorporates the
sensitive, sentimental nature of Julius as well as the active, heroic
characteristics of Guido. In this respect, Caecilia, admiring the
coarse, willful Guido as well as the gentle, sentimental Julius,
envisioned a composite of both to be "almost an ideal of mascu-

line perfection."[15] The father recognizes the heart of the conflict when he states that "Guido's honor clashes with Julius's love" and "Guido loves Blanca simply out of jealousy, because Julius loves her."[16] When, at the climax in the third act, Guido proposes that both renounce their claims on Blanca, Guido devises a method to save his honor, which is all that really matters. But Julius, the emotional and sensitive individual, cannot turn off his feelings, thus precipitating the catastrophe.

Less complex than his brother, Guido is a stilted and affected figure. Although he is depicted as a man of uncontrolled passion, his hate and scorn for Julius do not erupt from the depths of his soul, but are tempered by rational thought and express themselves in trenchant, ironic language. Guido's character has none of the demonic, fatalistic nature of Klinger's Guelfo, who runs about muttering incoherencies in the atmosphere of a foreboding twilight. All of Guido's actions are clearly but superficially motivated.

The Prince of Tarento, the father of the hostile brothers, in his conversations with his brother, the archbishop, reveals himself as the kindly, wise, and benevolent despot, who wishes to be a good father to his subjects as well as to his children. Clear, rational thinking determines his actions and lets him understand the basic conflict between his sons. But his reasoning shows its limitations when he believes that he can influence Julius to transfer his emotional feelings for Blanca to Caecilia. The Prince's final act, that of administering justice by stabbing Guido, the murderer of Julius, seems to be out of character. How could a father, who is the symbol of sanity and rational thinking, commit such a deed? To be sure, the crime of fratricide, perpetrated on his immediate family, has turned his well-ordered world into chaos. However, he does not kill his son in a moment of delirium, but after uttering a reflective soliloquy, in which he weighs his decision.

If in the scenes with the Prince and the Archbishop, Leisewitz directs mild satire against the Rationalists who would preserve the *status quo* at all costs, he employs the scenes at the convent to attack celibacy, as imposed by the church. Both the "Hainbund" and the "Stürmer und Dränger" stressed the free and natural expression of sex. Consequently, one of the chief targets was the institution of the church, which arbitrarily set up its rules of continence. When Julius, in his passionate ardor, calls at the convent to see Blanca, he successfully appeals to the human qualities of the mother superior herself. The latter, who had renounced worldly love nineteen years ago, is reminded by Julius' emotional entreaty of her former suitor, as she utters: "Oh, my Ricardo."[17] A little later on, the mother superior confesses to Blanca that "a saint (Heilige) is a beautiful aberration of nature."[18]

The mother superior's feelings pale when compared to those of Blanca. Her sensitive, emotional nature can not resist Julius' fervent proposal, and his kiss affects her so deeply that she falls into unconsciousness. When she comes to, she is a transformed person who dreams that she is in "the remotest corner of the earth—there is a small hut; space enough for embracing. There is a small field—space enough for vegetables and two graves; and then, Julius, eternity—space enough for love."[19] Upon learning that Julius was killed on his way to kidnap her, she breaks out of the convent and loses her mind at the sight of Julius' corpse. She reminds us of *Hamlet's* Ophelia. Theater audiences in the Storm and Stress period had become accustomed to the heroine becoming mentally deranged toward the end of the play, but it was novel to them to see her disturbed condition linked to the problem of asceticism in convent life. With respect to the religious overtones of *Julius von Tarent*, it must be mentioned that this drama, more than any other written in the age of genius, treats organized and orthodox Christianity. For the most part the Storm and Stress dramatists with whom we are concerned subscribed to an intensely personal and emotional religion which was divorced from dogmatic belief and religious practice.

Leisewitz's language and style also mark a sharp contrast to those of the writers discussed previously. Although we are told of the tempestuous state of the characters and find the dialogue liberally sprinkled with quotation marks, question marks, dashes, and short bursts of speech, the passions of the characters seem contrived and lack the elemental, demonic, compulsive quality of those engendered in Klinger's *Zwillinge*. Even though the stage directions call for a person to be "angry,"[20] "to run in with disheveled hair,"[21] or "to cry out,"[22] the individuals involved never actually seem to lose their composure. That a personage seldom seems overly perturbed is due in large measure to the

clear, logical way in which he expresses himself. As a protégé of
Lessing, Leisewitz uses a dialogue which is pithy, forceful, and
direct, reflecting logical and reasoned thought. That a character
of Leisewitz is totally conscious of his actions, even when beset
by intense emotional feelings, is brought out in Julius' conversation with Aspermonte, when he says: "Friend, even though I am
giddy with love, I still know that I am giddy."[23] Even Blanca, in
her deranged state, is fully conscious of her condition, when she
tells Caecilia "that it is a great misfortune to lose one's mind."[24]

Leisewitz' characters, like those of Lessing, like to engage in
lively, witty conversations flavored with dialectics, even when—
as applies to Leisewitz—such dialogues seem somewhat out of
character. A case in point is the initial conversation between
Julius and Blanca in the convent. On being reunited for the first
time after a long interval, the two erstwhile lovers could be expected to use a tender, heartfelt language, but instead they begin
with this clever, unemotional repartee:

JULIUS: O my Blanca!
BLANCA: Don't commit a sacrilege, Prince!
JULIUS: Don't commit perjury, Blanca!
BLANCA: No—for I hope to keep my word with heaven.
JULIUS: Your vows are an act of perjury. Can the second oath, even if
it was sworn to heaven, invalidate the first? What is meant by sworn
loyalty? A locked treasure, to which every thief has a key?[25]

Such dialogue is not unlike that of Grusche and Simon in Brecht's
Der kaukasische Kreidekreis, except that Brecht's reason for keeping the feelings of his lovers on ice is vitally related to his esthetic
theory of alienation.

The characters speak, for the most part, in a calm, rational,
imperturbable tone, even when Blanca dreams of her future love,
or when, in a deranged state, she speaks about the torments of
her soul; or when Guido laments his human lot and revolts
against the barriers that society has placed in his way. Even in
her madness, Blanca can reflect enough to view her lover's death
metaphorically as an universal experience: "Ah, that man crosses
the earth without leaving a trace, just as a smile passes over one's
face, or as the song of a bird goes through the forest."[26]

For dramatic effect, Leisewitz, like Klinger, employs contrasts,
although the polar opposites are not quite as accentuated, in
keeping with Leisewitz' more moderate temperament. It is ob-

vious that Leisewitz sets off Julius, the sentimental prince, against the ambitious and forceful brother; the two passionate sons, in turn, are contrasted with the enlightened father. The supersensitive Julius and Blanca are paired off with the coldly rational Aspermonte and Caecilia. Sometimes individuals themselves experience sudden turns of fortune. Blanca has become a bride of the church only to succumb to the power of earthly love; Caecilia, on the other hand, who has lost her lover, Julius, seeks the refuge of a cloister. Love and death, heaven and earth, stillness and tumult, madness and composure, wild craving and sentimental longing appear as antitheses which serve an integral esthetic function in the drama.

As a play written in the Aristotelian manner, *Julius von Tarent* is a carefully constructed piece of stagecraft. That Julius' death occurs already at the end of the fourth act seems incongruous, but Sidler points out that the fifth act is really a Classical tragedy in miniature; that it resolves itself into a conflict between the father and Guido, complete with ascending action, climax, and denouement.[27] In a drama where the characters are so carefully delineated, following the example set by Lessing, it is all the more difficult to conceive how a father who acts so calmly and deliberately could kill his own son. Perhaps it would have been better to have the rash and tempestuous Guido take his own life after seeing the blood on his hands.

The parade of people who come to view the corpse remind us of similar situations in *Ugolino* and *Die Zwillinge*. Leisewitz' scenes at the bier drip with sentiment, but they appealed to the contemporary theater audiences, who were accustomed to having their sensibilities and emotions preyed upon. Originally appearing on the stage in Berlin in 1776, Leisewitz' play was popular in the major German cities, with the leading actors relishing to play its roles.[28] The public preferred *Julius von Tarent* to *Die Zwillinge*, even though the latter play had been awarded the drama prize.

As already alluded to, young Schiller was infatuated with Leisewitz' play. An early work of his, *Cosmus von Medici*, which was later destroyed, was actually an imitation. In *Die Räuber* we find not only the same motif of the hostile brothers, but several instances of virtually literal echoes in text. *Kabale und Liebe* and *Die Braut von Messina* also contain passages which are strikingly similar to those in *Julius von Tarent*.[29] *Die Braut von Messina* obviously uses the same central motif, although it is deepened and ennobled by the Greek concept of fate.

CHAPTER 7

Conclusion

I N THIS STUDY of five dramatists of the Storm and Stress
period, we have devoted most space to Lenz because he is
most attuned to our times. There is a distinctly modern quality
about his characters, who are relentlessly buffeted about by powerful social and psychic forces until they lose their individuality
and become passive cynics. Brecht resurrected one of Lenz's
plays, which still occupy a prominent position in the repertory of
the German theater. Not only has the content of Lenz's dramas
had a strong influence on the contemporary stage, but their form
as well. Their episodic structure has been found ideally suited
through the method of repetition, to graphically depict man's
deterministic milieu. Gesture and mimetic art, as employed by
Lenz, have enabled the modern playwright to portray the human
being's predicament in situations where language no longer
suffices.

Although Wagner's dramas lack the depth of those of Lenz,
they are likewise concerned with social injustices perpetrated
by the privileged few on the lower classes. Better than any poet
of his age, Wagner was able to portray sympathetically, vividly,
and accurately the milieu of the common people. By placing his
characters in authentic situations, and by having them speak in
an unvarnished dialectal idiom, he was a precursor of the Naturalists, who were also concerned with presenting a slice of real
life to their audience.

Quite unjustly, Maler Müller has been more neglected by literary historians than any other dramatist of Storm and Stress.
His plays, we admit, are not stageworthy. *Faust* is in reality a
fragment, and *Golo und Genoveva* is too diffuse to be successful
on the stage. However, viewed purely as literature, both of these
works deserve a better reception than they have been accorded.
In *Faust* Müller gives fine poetic expression to the ebullient
young man of genius who would remove the shackles imposed
on him by fate and tradition in order to realize his potential.
Golo und Genoveva likewise strikes a personal note as it sensi-
tively unfolds a conflict between inclination and duty.

While Klinger's dramas are also a genuine expression of their author, it is by virtue of their form rather than their content that they achieve authenticity. Klinger's heroes, expressing themselves in a tense, emotionally charged idiom, unleash their instinctive and emotional feelings which, in turn, allow the characters to overcome their frustrations and experience their true selves. Influenced by the climate of Expressionism, literary scholars no longer regard Klinger's feverish outbursts as bombastic, ridiculous, and pathological manifestations, but as healthy expressions of an individual seeking to come to terms with a problematic universe. The use of parody, caricature, and grotesquerie in dramas such as *Simsone Grisaldo* and *Sturm und Drang* prefigures similar modern artistic devices to reveal man's disharmonious state.

In the traditional sense, Leisewitz' drama, *Julius von Tarent,* is the most carefully constructed play of those included in our study, but it is, at the same time, the least satisfying insofar as catching the true spirit of Storm and Stress is concerned. The characters are so logical in their manner of expression and thinking that their passionate and emotional outbursts, when they do occur, seem contrived and out of place. Leisewitz illustrates all too well that Rationalism and the Storm and Stress were two opposing schools of thought that could not be integrated.

In restrospect, the revolutionary period of the Storm and Stress was initially a revolt against the outmoded age of Enlightenment. During its short duration, it developed a program of its own and inspired bold new artistic creations which were to infuse fresh spirit and new ideas into subsequent literary movements.

Notes and References

Chapter One

1. *Herders Sämmtliche Werke,* ed. B. Suphan (Berlin, 1891), V, 204–6.
2. Johann Georg Hamann, *Sämmtliche Werke,* ed. J. Nadler (Vienna, 1949), II, 208.
3. *Ibid.,* II, 75.
4. *Werke,* V, 209–10.
5. *Der junge Goethe,* ed. H. F. Lamberg (Berlin, 1966), III, 106. A new edition of Max Morris' collection.
6. *Ibid.,* II, 257. Letter from Herder, dated July 10, 1772.

Chapter Two

1. *Briefe von und an J. M. R. Lenz,* ed. K. Freye and W. Stammler (Leipzig, 1918), I, 103. Hereafter cited as *Briefe.*
2. *Briefe,* I, 114.
3. *Ibid.,* 29.
4. Erich Schmidt, *Lenz und Klinger* (Berlin, 1878), p. 16.
5. *Goethe-Gedenkausgabe,* ed. E. Beutler (Zürich, 1964), zweiter Ergänzungsband, p. 29. Hereafter cited as *Tagebücher.*
6. Heinz Kindermann, *Lenz und die deutsche Romantik* (Berlin, 1925), p. 194.
7. J. M. R. Lenz, *Gesammelte Schriften,* ed. Franz Blei (Munich, 1909), I, 251. Hereafter cited as *Schriften.*
8. *Ibid.,* p. 234.
9. *Ibid.,* p. 252.
10. *Ibid.,* p. 244.
11. *Ibid.,* p. 238.
12. M. N. Rosanow, *Jakob M. R. Lenz* (Leipzig, 1909), p. 153.
13. *Schriften,* I, 235.
14. *Ibid.,* p. 237.
15. *Briefe,* I, 59.
16. Rosanow, p. 195.
17. H. B. Garland, *Storm and Stress* (London, 1952), p. 63.
18. Karl S. Guthke, *Geschichte und Poetik der deutschen Tragikomödie* (Göttingen, 1961), p. 63.
19. *Schriften,* I, 344.
20. *Ibid.,* p. 330.
21. *Ibid.,* p. 333.
22. *Ibid.,* pp. 359–60.
23. Wolfgang Stammler, "'Der Hofmeister' von J. M. R. Lenz" (diss. Halle, 1908), p. 24.
24. Roy Pascal, *The German Sturm und Drang* (New York, 1953), p. 70.

25. Max Spalter, *Brecht's Tradition* (Baltimore, 1967), p. 14.
26. *Schriften*, I, 399.
27. Spalter, p. 14.
28. F. J. Schneider, *Die deutsche Dichtung der Geniezeit* (Stuttgart, 1952), p. 207.
29. Spalter, p. 16.
30. *Schriften*, I, 358.
31. *Schriften*, III, 53.
32. *Briefe*, I, 191.
33. *Schriften*, III, 92.
34. *Ibid.*, p. 32.
35. *Ibid.*, p. 34.
36. *Ibid.*, p. 45.
37. *Ibid.*, pp. 55–57.
38. *Ibid.*, pp. 39–42.
39. *Ibid.*, pp. 58–59.
40. *Ibid.*, p. 53.
41. *Ibid.*, p. 59.
42. *Ibid.*, p. 53.
43. *Ibid.*, p. 40.
44. *Ibid.*, p. 53.
45. *Ibid.*, p. 53.
46. *Ibid.*, p. 40.
47. *Ibid.*, p. 66.
48. Werner Wien, "Lenzens Sturm und Drang-Dramen innerhalb seiner religiösen Entwicklung" (diss. Göttingen, 1935), p. 140.
49. Wien, p. 123.
50. *Schriften*, III, 86.
51. Cf. *Schriften*, III, 87, 90–91.
52. *Schriften*, III, 71.
53. *Ibid.*, p. 81.
54. *Ibid.*, p. 70.
55. *Ibid.*, p. 72.
56. *Ibid.*, p. 92.
57. *Ibid.*, p. 70.
58. *Ibid.*, p. 81.
59. *Ibid.*, p. 76.
60. *Ibid.*, II, 330.
61. *Briefe*, I, 115.
62. Rosanow, pp. 224–30.
63. *Schriften*, II, 268.
64. *Ibid.*, p. 269.
65. *Ibid.*, p. 262.
66. *Ibid.*, pp. 274–77.

67. *Ibid.*, pp. 307–8.
68. *Ibid.*, p. 254.
69. *Ibid.*, p. 294.
70. Walter Hinck, *Das deutsche Lustspiel des 17. und 18. Jahrhunderts und die italienische Komödie* (Stuttgart, 1965), pp. 338–39.
71. *Schriften*, II, 291.
72. *Ibid.*, p. 268.
73. *Ibid.*, p. 322.
74. *Ibid.*, p. 318.
75. *Ibid.*, pp. 304–6.
76. Hinck, p. 445.

Chapter Three

1. Schneider, p. 214.
2. *Gedenkausgabe*, X, 658.
3. Erich Schmidt, *Heinrich Leopold Wagner*, 2nd ed. (Jena, 1879), pp. 18–19.
4. *Ibid.*, pp. 22, 144–53.
5. *Ibid.*, pp. 48–51.
6. *Ibid.*, p. 22.
7. *Goethes Werke*, Weimar edition, 1 Abt., Vol. 38, p. 422.
8. *Sturm und Drang. Dramatische Schriften*, ed. Erich Loewenthal. Two vols. (Heidelberg, 1949), II, 477.
9. *Schriften*, II, 498.
10. *Ibid.*, pp. 505–6.
11. *Ibid.*, p. 473.
12. *Ibid.*, p. 471.
13. *Ibid.*, p. 487.
14. *Ibid.*, p. 488.
15. *Ibid.*, p. 489.
16. *Ibid.*, p. 510.
17. *Ibid.*, p. 492.
18. Schmidt, p. 65.
19. *Schriften*, II, 490.
20. *Ibid.*, p. 497.
21. *Ibid.*, p. 520.
22. *Ibid.*, p. 518.
23. *Ibid.*, p. 526.
24. Schneider, p. 215.
25. It appeared in Frankfurt in 1779 under the title *Evchen Humbrecht oder Ihr Mütter merkts euch*. See J. M. Rameckers, "Der Kindesmord in der Literatur der Sturm-und-Drang-Periode" (diss. Amsterdam, 1927), p. 178.
26. Rameckers, p. 178.

27. Hermann Hettner, *Geschichte der deutschen Literatur im achtzehnten Jahrhundert.* Reissue (Berlin, 1961), II, 208–9.

28. *Schriften,* II, 551.

29. *Ibid.,* p. 580.

30. *Ibid.,* p. 605.

31. *Ibid.,* p. 565.

32. *Ibid.,* p. 592.

33. *Ibid.,* pp. 566–67.

34. *Ibid.,* p. 605.

Chapter Four

1. "Lied eines bluttrunkenen Wodanadlers."

2. Bernhard Seuffert, *Maler Müller,* 2nd ed. (Berlin, 1881), p. 24.

3. Seuffert, p. 25.

4. *Briefe,* I, 231.

5. Incomplete, it was written about the same time as the other idylls, but was only published in the twentieth century: *Maler Müllers Idyllen,* complete ed. by O. Heuer. Three vols. (Leipzig, 1914).

6. *Sturm und Drang: Dramatische Schriften,* ed. E. Loewenthal. Two vols. (Heidelberg, 1949), II, 362. Hereafter cited as Loewenthal.

7. F. A. Schmidt, "Maler Müllers dramatisches Schaffen unter besonderer Berücksichtigung seiner Faust Dichtungen" (diss. Göttingen, 1936), p. 46. Cf. Seuffert, p. 178.

8. Loewenthal, II, 362.

9. Maler Müller, *Situation aus Fausts Leben* in *Stürmer und Dränger,* ed. A. Sauer (Deutsche National-Litteratur), Vol. 81, p. 169. Hereafter cited as Sauer.

10. Schmidt, p. 53.

11. C. F. D. Schubart, "*Situation aus Fausts Leben* von Mahler Müller," *Deutsche Chronik,* ed. C. F. D. Schubart (Ulm: C. U. Wagner), 32. Stück (1776), pp. 253-55.

12. Loewenthal, II, 368.

13. *Ibid.,* pp. 367–68.

14. *Ibid.,* p. 428.

15. Fritz Strich, *Die Mythologie in der deutschen Literatur von Klopstock bis Wagner* (Halle, 1910), p. 244.

16. Loewenthal, II, 378.

17. Schmidt, p. 80.

18. Seuffert, p. 188.

19. Cf. Wagner (*Reue nach der Tat*), Goethe (*Judenpredigt*), Lenz (*Soldaten*), and Achim von Arnim (*Halle und Jerusalem*).

20. Loewenthal, II, 433.

21. Friedrich Schlegel, "Ueber Mahler Müllers Werke," *Deutsches Museum,* ed. Friedrich Schlegel (Wien, 1813), IV, 252.

22. *Allgemeine Deutsche Biographie,* XXII, 532.

23. Cf. Loewenthal, II, 626.
24. Seuffert, p. 185.
25. Schmidt, p. 137.
26. Hettner, II, 217.
27. Friedrich Gundolf, *Shakespeare und der deutsche Geist* (Berlin, 1911), p. 263.
28. P. Krech, "Die Rolle der Natur im Sturm und Drang-Drama" (diss. Erlangen, 1929), p. 105.
29. Sauer, p. 17.
30. *Ibid.*, p. 53.
31. *Ibid.*, p. 109.
32. *Ibid.*, p. 159.
33. *Ibid.*, p. 59.
34. *Ibid.*, p. 115.
35. *Ibid.*, p. 134.
36. Schmidt, p. 139 and footnote.

Chapter Five

1. *Friedrich Maximilian Klingers dramatische Jungendwerke,* ed. by Hans Berendt and Kurt Wolff. Three vols. (Leipzig, 1912), I, xx. Hereafter cited as *Jugendwerke.*
2. *Goethes Werke,* Weimarer Ausgabe Abt. I, Vol. 28, p. 253.
3. Max Rieger, *Klinger in der Sturm und Drang-Periode* (Darmstadt, 1880), p. 380. The appendix to this book contains important Klinger letters. These letters will be cited henceforth as: Rieger (*Briefe*).
4. Rieger (*Briefe*), p. 387.
5. *Ibid.*, p. 391.
6. *Ibid.*, p. 397.
7. *Goethes Werke,* WA, Abt. IV, Vol. 3, p. 110.
8. Rieger (*Briefe*), p. 419.
9. *Ibid.*, pp. 422–23.
10. *Jugendwerke,* I, 351–52.
11. Rieger (*Briefe*), p. 373.
12. *Jugendwerke,* I, 233.
13. *Ibid.*, p. 241.
14. *Ibid.*, p. 286.
15. *Ibid.*, p. 272.
16. *Ibid.*, p. 237.
17. *Ibid.*, p. 252.
18. *Ibid.*, p. 252.
19. *Ibid.*, p. 304.
20. *Ibid.*, p. 304.

21. *Ibid.*, pp. 319–20.

22. *Ibid.*, pp. 309–10.

23. *Ibid.*, p. 249.

24. Kurt May, "Beitrag zur Phänomenologie des Dramas im Sturm und Drang," *Germanisch-Romanische Monatsschrift*, XVIII (1930), 266.

25. Garland, pp. 79–80.

26. *Briefe von und an Gottfried August Bürger*, ed. A. Strodtmann. Four vols. (Berlin, 1874), III, 1.

27. Hettner, II, 200.

28. Cf. p. 125.

29. Karl Philipp Moritz, *Anton Reiser*, ed. Ludwig Geiger (*Deutsche Litteraturdenkmale des 18. und 19. Jahrhunderts*), Vol. 23, p. 302.

30. Christoph Hering, *Friedrich Maximilian Klinger* (Berlin, 1966), pp. 79–80.

31. *Goethes Werke, Weimarer Ausgabe*, Abt. I, Vol. 28, p. 253.

32. Rieger (*Briefe*), p. 385.

33. *Ibid.*, pp. 385–86.

34. *Ibid.*, p. 388.

35. *Jugendwerke*, II, 205.

36. *Ibid.*, p. 174.

37. *Ibid.*, p. 200.

38. Luise Kolb, *Klingers "Simsone Grisaldo"* (Halle, 1929), pp. 98–103. In her work, Miss Kolb makes a good case for the influence of Shaftesbury on Klinger.

39. *Jugendwerke*, II, 131.

40. *Ibid.*, p. 155.

41. *Ibid.*, p. 245.

42. *Ibid.*, p. 157.

43. *Ibid.*, pp. 190–91.

44. *Ibid.*, p. 196.

45. *Ibid.*, p. 192.

46. *Ibid.*, p. 249.

47. *Ibid.*, p. 250.

48. *Ibid.*, p. 259.

49. *Ibid.*, p. 232.

50. *Ibid.*, p. 233.

51. *Ibid.*, p. 234.

52. Cf. p. 136.

53. *Jugendwerke*, II, 192.

54. *Ibid.*, p. 185.

55. *Ibid.*, pp. 239–40.

56. *Ibid.*, p. 132.

57. *Ibid.*, p. 158.
58. *Ibid.*, p. 247.
59. Cf. p. 105.
60. Rieger (*Briefe*), p. 399.
61. *Ibid.*, p. 394.
62. *Ibid.*, p. 398.
63. *Ibid.*, p. 397.
64. *Ibid.*, p. 394.
65. *Ibid.*, p. 398.
66. *Jugendwerke*, II, 270.
67. *Ibid.*, p. 269.
68. *Ibid.*, p. 299.
69. *Ibid.*, p. 339.
70. Rieger (*Briefe*), pp. 197–98.
71. *Jugendwerke*, II, 284.
72. *Ibid.*, p. 284.
73. *Ibid.*, p. 340.
74. Rieger (*Briefe*), p. 198.
75. Fritz Brüggemann, "Klingers Sturm und Drang," *Zeitschrift für deutsche Bildung*, II (1926), 205.
76. Hering, pp. 97–98.
77. *Jugendwerke*, II, 265–66.
78. *Ibid.*, pp. 315–16.

Chapter Six

1. Gregor Kutschera von Aichbergen, *Johann Anton Leisewitz* (Wien, 1876), p. 16.
2. *Ibid.*, p. 15.
3. *Ibid.*, p. 32.
4. *Tagebücher*, p. 106.
5. Kutschera, p. 45.
6. Hettner, II, 272–73.
7. *Ibid.*, cf. footnote on p. 272.
8. E. H. Zeydel, "Neues zu Leisewitzens *Julius von Tarent*," *Zeitschrift für deutsche Philologie*, LVI (1931), 439.
9. J. A. Leisewitz, *Julius von Tarent* in *Stürmer und Dränger*, ed. A. Sauer, Deutsche National-Litteratur, Vol. 79, p. 319. Hereafter cited as Sauer.
10. Sauer, p. 329.
11. *Ibid.*, pp. 340–41.
12. *Ibid.*, p. 341.
13. *Ibid.*, p. 340.
14. Kutschera, p. 97.

15. Sauer, p. 331.
16. *Ibid.*, p. 329.
17. *Ibid.*, p. 334.
18. *Ibid.*, p.356.
19. *Ibid.*, p. 338.
20. *Ibid.*, p. 368.
21. *Ibid.*, p. 369.
22. *Ibid.*, p. 371.
23. *Ibid.*, p. 321.
24. *Ibid.*, p. 371.
25. *Ibid.*, pp. 334–35.
26. *Ibid.*, p. 370.
27. Josef Sidler, *J. A. Leisewitz, Julius von Tarent* (Zürich, 1966), pp. 50–51.
28. Kutschera, pp. 74–75.
29. *Ibid.*, pp. 95–98.

Selected Bibliography

1. Anthologies of Storm and Stress Literature
Stürmer und Dränger, ed. A. SAUER. *Deutsche National-Litteratur*, vols. 79–80–81. Berlin, 1883.
Sturm und Drang, ed. K. FREYE. Bongs Klassiker. 4 vols. Berlin, 1911.
Sturm und Drang. Dramatische Schriften, ed. E. LOEWENTHAL. 2 vols. Heidelberg, 1949.

2. General Studies.
GARLAND, H. B. *Storm and Stress*. London, 1952.
GUNDOLF, F. *Shakespeare und der deutsche Geist*. Berlin, 1911.
HETTNER, H. *Geschichte der deutschen Literatur im achtzehnten Jahrhundert*. Reissue Berlin, 1961.
KINDERMANN, H. *Die Entwicklung der Sturm und Drang-Bewegung*. Vienna, 1925.
KORFF, H. A. *Geist der Goethezeit*, Vol. I: *Sturm und Drang*. Leipzig, 1923.
MELCHINGER, S. *Dramaturgie des Sturm und Drangs*. Gotha, 1929.
PASCAL, R. *The German Sturm und Drang*. New York, 1953.
SCHNEIDER, F. J. *Die deutsche Dichtung der Geniezeit*. Stuttgart, 1952.

3. Lenz
LENZ, J. M. R. *Gesammelte Schriften*, ed. FRANZ BLEI. 5 vols. Munich, 1909–13.
Briefe von und an J. M. R. Lenz, ed. K. FREYE and W. STAMMLER. Two vols. Leipzig, 1918.
GRUPPE, O. F. *Reinhold Lenz, Leben und Werke*. Berlin, 1861.
GUTHKE, K. S. *Geschichte und Poetik der deutschen Tragikomödie*. Göttingen, 1961.
HINCK, W. *Das deutsche Lustspiel des 17. und 18. Jahrhunderts und die italienische Komödie*. Stuttgart, 1965.
HOLLERER, W. "Lenz–Die Soldaten," *Das deutsche Drama*, ed. BENNO VON WIESE. Düsseldorf, 1964, I, 128–47.
KINDERMANN, H. *Lenz und die deutsche Romantik*. Berlin, 1925.
ROSANOW, M. N. *Jakob M. R. Lenz*. Leipzig, 1909.
SCHMIDT, ERICH. *Lenz und Klinger*. Berlin, 1878.
SPALTER, MAX. *Brecht's Tradition*. Baltimore, 1967.
STAMMLER, W. " 'Der Hofmeister' von J. M. R. Lenz." Diss. Halle, 1908.
WIEN, W. "Lenzens Sturm und Drang-Dramen innerhalb seiner religiösen Entwicklung." Diss. Göttingen, 1935.

4. Wagner

Sturm und Drang. Dramatische Schriften, ed. E. Loewenthal. Volume II contains *Die Reue nach der Tat* and *Die Kindsmörderin.*

Rameckers, J. M. "Der Kindesmord in der Literatur der Sturm und Drang-Periode." Diss. Amsterdam, 1927.

Froitzheim, J. *Goethe und H. L. Wagner.* Strassburg, 1889.

Schmidt, Erich. *Heinrich Leopold Wagner,* 2nd ed. Jena, 1879. Includes important letters.

5. Maler Müller

Sturm und Drang. Dramatische Schriften, ed. E. Loewenthal. Vol. II contains *Fausts Leben* and *Fausts Spazierfahrt.*

Stürmer und Dränger, ed. A. Sauer. *Deutsche National-Litteratur,* Vol. 81, contains *Golo und Genoveva* and *Situation aus Fausts Leben.*

Denk, F. *Friedrich Müller, der Malerdichter und Dichtermaler.* Speyer, 1930.

Luntowsky, A. *Maler Müller.* Leipzig, 1908.

Schmidt, F. A. "Maler Müllers dramatisches Schaffen unter besonderer Berücksichtigung seiner Faust-Dichtungen." Diss. Göttingen, 1936.

Seuffert, B. *Maler Müller,* 2nd ed. Berlin, 1881.

6. Klinger

Friedrich Maximilian Klingers dramatische Jugendwerke, ed. Hans Berendt and Kurt Wolff. Three vols. Leipzig, 1912.

Bruggemann, Fritz. "Klingers Sturm und Drang," *Zeitschrift für deutsche Bildung,* II (1926), 196–208.

Hering, Christoph. *Friedrich Maximilian Klinger.* Berlin, 1966.

Kolb, Luise. *Klingers "Simsone Grisaldo."* Halle, 1929.

Kurz, Werner. *F. M. Klingers "Sturm und Drang."* Halle, 1913.

Rieger, Max. *Klinger in der Sturm und Drang-Periode.* Darmstadt, 1880. The appendix to this book contains important Klinger letters.

Schmidt, Erich. *Lenz und Klinger.* Berlin, 1878.

7. Leisewitz

Stürmer und Dränger, ed. A. Sauer. *Deutsche National-Litteratur,* Vol. 79, contains *Julius von Tarent.*

Kuhlhorn, W. *Leisewitzens "Julius von Tarent."* Halle, 1912.

Kutschera von Aichbergen, Gregor. *Johann Anton Leisewitz.* Viena, 1876.

Sidler, Josef. *J. A. Leisewitz, "Julius von Tarent."* Zürich, 1966.

Zeydel, E. H. "Neues zu Leisewitzens *Julius von Tarent,*" *Zeitschrift für deutsche Philologie,* LVI (1931), 436–44.

Index

169